Boys Will Read | Parent Series, Book 1

BOYS AND BOOKS

What You Need to Know and Do
So Your 9- to 14-Year-Old Son Will Read

HILLARY TUBIN

BOYS AND BOOKS
What You Need to Know and Do
So Your 9- to 14-Year-Old Son Will Read

ISBN-13: 978-0-9975749-0-6 Paperback
ISBN-13: 978-0-9975749-1-3 eBook

DISCLAIMER: The information in this book is intended for educational and informational purposes only. It should not be treated as advice or substitute for seeking help from a qualified professional. If advice concerning reading disabilities or related matters is needed, the services of a qualified professional should be sought.

Names and details of the persons presented in the book have been changed to protect their privacy. The people and events described and depicted in this book are for educational purposes only.

Cover Designer: Thor Svartefoss
Editor and Interior Design: Sara Zibrat

Library of Congress Control Number: 2016907399

Publisher's Cataloging-In-Publication Data
(Prepared by The Donohue Group, Inc.)

Names: Tubin, Hillary.
Title: Boys and books : what you need to know and do so your 9- to 14-year-old son will read / Hillary Tubin.
Description: Darien, CT : B-R Publishing, [2016] | Series: Boys will read. Parent series ; book 1 | Includes bibliographical references.
Identifiers: LCCN 2016907399 | ISBN 978-0-9975749-0-6 (paperback) | ISBN 978-0-9975749-1-3 (ebook)
Subjects: LCSH: Boys--Books and reading. | Reading--Parent participation. | Reading promotion.
Classification: LCC LB1050.2 .T83 2016 | DDC 649/.58--dc23

Published by B-R Publishing
Darien, CT
USA
This paper meets the requirements of ANSI/NISO 239.48-1992 (Permanence of Paper).

❧ DEDICATION ❧

To all the boys I had the privilege of teaching literacy (as Miss Cohen, Ms. E and Ms. T), who pushed me out of my reading comfort zone and graciously and enthusiastically showed me there's more than one way to engage with a book

In memory of Dr. Lawrence (Larry) Sipe, who showed me how to appreciate the way boys read and respond to books

⁓ FREE BONUSES ⁓

As a thank you for buying this book, I have included a link to a comprehensive workbook in the section RoadMap: The 10 Building Blocks, plus a free resource link at the end of each building block.

Visit the link below to download the **complete bonus package**. This resource includes all the bonus material in one place.

www.hillarytubin.com/freecompletebonuspackage

❧ TABLE OF CONTENTS ❧

ঞ INTRODUCTION: Becoming Boy-Responsive ঞ

"Reading is boring and stupid... There aren't any books I like to read... I want to play video games... Only nerds and girls read books, and I play sports!"

Do any of these remarks—typically uttered by boys when they are asked to read a book for pleasure—sound familiar?

If you answered, "Yes!" you are not alone.

Three recent national surveys found a large majority of preteen and early teen boys aren't reading in their spare time.

Scholastic's 2015 Kids & Family Reading Report showed that, when asked, **76%** of preteen and early teen boys responded that they don't read for fun every day.[1]

The 2015 Common Sense Media national survey stated that **73%** of 8- to 12-year-olds and **81%** of 13- to 18-year-olds don't read for fun every day.[2]

The 2015 NAEP reading survey results confirmed Scholastic's and the Common Sense Media findings, with **81%** of eighth graders reporting they don't frequently read for fun, either.[3]

That's because boys and books are like oil and water. It doesn't matter how much shaking, stirring, hoping or wishing takes place, they just don't mix together on their own.

There's a word for boys and books not mixing together: **aliteracy**.

Not illiteracy (the inability to read), but aliteracy: the state of being able to read, knowing how to read, but choosing *not* to read. Too many boys today easily fit this definition—most likely your son, too—and the long-term effects of the non-reading behavior are now becoming obvious and troubling.[4]

On its most recent international reading literacy assessment, PISA (the Program for International Student Assessment) found that 15-year-old boys from the United States ranked 23rd in the world, a full 75 points below the top-ranked country (38 PISA points is equivalent to nearly 10 months of school, meaning US boys are about two grade levels behind the front-runner). This is troublesome because reading literacy is not about regurgitating what was read. Instead, PISA's assessment expected boys to understand, think about, and *use* what they read. A large percentage were unable to meet the challenge, and many also self-reported that they didn't read books in their spare time at all.[5]

Additionally, a well-regarded research study found that frequent reading for pleasure in childhood is directly linked to substantial cognitive growth between the ages of 10 and 16, and also contributed to continued learning and vocabulary growth as an adult. This means that when boys aren't reading outside of school, they miss out on fully developing and strengthening the thinking and vocabulary skills that are necessary for both their short-term and long-term achievement.[6]

Now, more than ever, it is crucial for preteen and early teen boys to engage with reading in order to successfully participate in today's ever-changing, more complex, global, and knowledge-based world. Brushing aside boys' aversion to reading with a wave of one's hand and the catch-all dismissal, "Boys don't like to read," just isn't adequate to prepare them for the life they will need to live.

Too many boys' futures are at stake. They need reading in order to become successful in their lives, but they can't do it alone. They need someone to show them that reading books for pleasure can be a very enjoyable way to learn about anything they are interested in and, in the process, become the best version of themselves.

Right now, however, self-proclaimed non-reading boys are making a choice, but is it an informed choice? Do they have any idea of the mental and cognitive consequences of their decision and how that will play out in their future lives? Do they even realize there's another way of looking at pleasure reading—as a tool for self-learning and for taking control of their destiny?

The answer is a resounding NO, but all is not lost.

Add detergent to oil and water, and voilà! They blend. The same happens with boys and books. Add an aware and knowledgeable adult (who also has a plan) to the mix, and it becomes possible for boys to **re-define their relationship to reading** and make better, more informed choices for their lives.

"The man who does not read good books has no advantage over the man who cannot read."—Mark Twain

WHO'S RESPONSIBLE TO HELP BOYS AND BOOKS MIX

In a perfect world, everyone (policy makers, schools and parents) would work together in harmony, and each would shoulder the responsibility to help aliterate preteen and early teen boys change their attitude toward reading and to develop their relationship with books. However, it's far from a perfect world, and right now nobody is in the driver's seat on this issue.

Policy makers are currently focusing on three things: Science, Technology, Engineering and Math (STEM), early childhood reading, and standardized testing/accountability for teachers and schools. Two of those three are bringing about very positive results, but not for preteen and early teen boys and reading.

Focusing on STEM has helped girls change their perception of math and science. The work being done is influencing girls' math achievement and is closing the gap that has stood between girls and boys for the past 40 years. In some places, girls are now surpassing boys in both math and science, but because literacy's been relatively neglected over the last few years, even girls' performance in reading is starting to suffer.[7]

Focusing on early childhood reading has created very positive results, too. More students are mastering their reading skills and, even though there is still a gap between boys and girls when they reach 9 years of age, that gap has significantly closed.[8] Unfortunately, funding for reading typically doesn't extend past the third grade.

The Red Herring

By focusing on standardized testing and accountability, policy makers created a dangerous "red herring" that's misleading and is distracting everyone from the scariest, most difficult challenge facing society today: the gender reading gap that still persists for teenage boys and the serious implications of that condition.

While the math/science achievement gap steadily closes between boys and girls, the reading achievements of middle- and high-school boys are not changing.[9] They continue to stagnate. As they move up through the grades, these boys are unable to take the reading skills that they had developed by third grade and use them to understand grade-level complex texts with proficiency. What this translates to is that they fall further and further behind in their scholastic development. Their intellectual growth is effectively shut down and they "drop out" of active participation, even if they continue to attend classes.

More standardized testing is NOT the answer to improving boys' reading achievement! There is no research that supports this policy. If anything, all of the standardized testing that is forced on preteen and early teen boys today only exacerbates the aliteracy problem in our country. It certainly does not improve it.

Where's Reading for Pleasure in Schools?

Presently, schools' hands are tied. Due to the high-stakes testing of the Common Core/state reading standards (with school funding being tied to accountability measures), what passes for "reading" in many schools focuses on test prep material (worksheets and computer programs) and close reading of short complex texts.

Reading performance has become re-defined as proficiency on standardized tests and the accumulation of English credits, with the hope that it will lead to college- and career-ready seniors who are prepared to take on the world.

Hoping that this antiquated view of reading would do the trick has proved disastrous. A new study that was just released found that only 8% of 2013's high school graduates achieved the readiness goal, even though many of the other 92% received diplomas and were attending college.[10]

This study confirmed that just showing up at school and only doing what's necessary to pass a class and be proficient on a standardized test does not make one ready for the world, and definitely not the world that is waiting for preteen and early teen boys to enter it.

For many that are in charge of our educational systems, reading for pleasure is no longer a priority and has a negative connotation; they believe it's not rigorous enough. Sadly, this short-sighted view creates a Catch-22 situation. If they don't first develop a pleasure reading habit, boys will never be able to read the complex texts expected of them later on.

Reading for Pleasure at Home

Another problem is lack of funding, time and support for pleasure reading to take place in the schools. Instead, many elementary and middle school teachers and administrators rely on the boys' home environment to be responsible for preteen and early teen boys' reading habits. In today's educational landscape, it's become the only place that 9- to-14-year-old boys are reading for fun.

The problem with this thinking is that—at home—most boys choose to do *everything but* read for pleasure, unless it's mandatory and forced upon them. Even trying to get them to read books for school is a battle. Parents are now expected to encourage the reading habit at home, but without any kind of support or instruction on how to do that, they're struggling or simply giving up on even trying.

Unfortunately, the home reading habit is the only kind of reading that will substantially strengthen boys' cognitive skills and stamina (the ability to sustain prolonged mental effort), build their vocabulary, and significantly improve their reading achievement.

This then leads to the question, **"Who's responsible for working with parents on how to instill the reading habit at home with their preteen and early teen sons?"**

The answer: nobody is responsible. That's why I left teaching to write the *Boys Will Read | Parent Series*. Its purpose is to provide instruction, guidance, support and encouragement to frustrated parents of self-proclaimed non-reading preteen and early teen boys when they have no one else to turn to. I know what's possible, and I want to share it with you.

WHAT'S POSSIBLE: Boys' Reading Can Be Re-shaped at Home

I spent 20+ years as a literacy educator and helped more than 350 boys transform their reading habit. For 10 years, I taught literacy to boys ages 9–11 in a suburban school district, and then for 10 more years, I taught literacy to boys ages 11–14 in an urban school district.

Here's what I discovered: No matter where I taught, or the particular details of their lives, there was one common denominator that many boys shared when they entered my classroom every September: the lack of a daily reading habit. No one was immune.

Addresses and zip codes didn't protect them. High IQ scores didn't protect them. Race, ethnicity and/or religion didn't protect them. Traveling, visiting museums, or playing a musical instrument didn't protect them. And surprisingly, their parent's college degrees didn't protect them either.

Most boys I taught between the ages of 9 and 14 had "the skills to read, but not the will to read" outside of school, even if their parents wanted them to. Even if *I* wanted them to.

Because *wanting* them to wasn't enough.

Aliterate preteen and early teen boys needed something very different (so that they would choose to read on their own because they wanted to), so I went on a quest to find out exactly what would make that possible.

I read, researched, observed sports coaches who my boys responded to, talked to the boys themselves, took classes, and immersed myself in a lot of trial and error. Each year, I learned more about bringing boys and books together and I thought I had it figured out: Stop being their teacher and instead instill the reading habit by becoming what I call their ***reading habit coach***.

Then I changed jobs.

For the last 10 years of my career, I taught literacy to 11- to 14-year-old boys for a three-year span—from September of sixth grade until June of eighth grade.

My principal fully endorsed middle school boys reading real books as a viable way for them to become proficient readers. She trusted me and provided the space, support and resources needed for success. However, having access to plenty of books and being their reading habit coach wasn't enough for this age group. Both helped, but aliteracy held on tighter and longer with older boys. They needed more.

A new quest began.

The Power of Parents

My biggest "a-ha!" moments and greatest learning occurred when I became a graduate student in the Reading/Writing/Literacy Master's degree program at the University of Pennsylvania. As I dug deeply into my studies, I also conducted research to better understand early teen boys, their brain/age/grade (BAG) needs, and their relationship to reading and books. I also studied to become a reading specialist, in order to expand my knowledge on what works best for boys who struggle with reading.

After I graduated, I still was not satisfied with what I knew, so I continued my quest by becoming a National Board Certified Teacher in Early Adolescence/English Language Arts. This rigorous and challenging process took my thinking about boys and books to a new level, and that's what I want to share with you today.

Through my hands-on research, I discovered that—far more than was true for 9- to 11-year old boys—early teen boys needed their parent's support and encouragement at home in order to read for pleasure. I was only rarely able to successfully instill the reading habit without a boy's parent(s)' direct support of his reading for pleasure at home. My influence as a boy's teacher was definitely secondary to that of a boy's parents or someone significant in his family or home.

For boys of this age, I learned how important it was that their teachers and parents worked together to help them re-shape their relationship to reading and to use their spare time to read.

It was my responsibility in school to ensure that boys had the grade-appropriate reading skills and were prepared for the kinds of reading they would be required to do in their adult lives. However, without their parents stepping up and supporting their reading for pleasure at home, it didn't happen. It couldn't happen.

Parents are the critical ingredient needed to mix boys and books so that they will read for pleasure. Teachers can help support parents, but the 30-minutes-a-day reading habit will only thrive and survive if it is instilled at home.

Being Boy-Responsive

Over the years, while I was working with boys and their parents on how to develop the daily habit of reading for pleasure at home, I began to notice a very distinct pattern unfold. Aliterate boys whose parents were supportive and responsive to their unique/specific reading needs and *committed* to creating the reading environment they needed (even if it was uncomfortable and/or inconvenient) became readers.

In contrast, aliterate boys whose parents were unable/unwilling to meet their sons where they were—who wouldn't or couldn't create the necessary reading environment at home—didn't become readers.

Eventually, I put my finger on the 10 non-negotiable fundamental actions that needed to be in place at home before early teen boys would be willing to even think about transforming their habit of not reading into one where they would read regularly.

The best news is that I discovered that *any* parent could develop the mindset and create the reading environment if they were committed and willing to buy in to the program, let go of their prior patterns of thinking and behavior, and give the ideas a chance.

I now call these non-negotiable fundamental actions the **10 Building Blocks.** Your willingness to cultivate and use them for your son is what I call being **boy-responsive**. The first five building blocks develop the **boy-responsive *reading mindset*** that parents must have in place before they can then create the **boy-responsive *reading environment*** by developing the last five building blocks.

The bottom line is that your son needs you. By himself, he can't transform his non-reading habit into a reading habit, but with you making it possible for him, he can. I *know* this. I've seen it happen.

Reading for pleasure is a foundation for his success in every aspect of his life, and success builds upon success, with far-reaching consequences for his ability to cope and survive in a rapidly changing world.

Right now, the choice is yours.

You can either keep reading this book, commit to developing the 10 Building Blocks, and watch your son thrive, or you can keep doing what you're doing.

It's your decision, but I do hope you will join me in this effort to create better prospects for your son. Together, we'll help him change his relationship to reading so that he thrives in the future.

❧ ROADMAP: Developing the 10 Building Blocks ❧

I'm so glad you joined me! Your son is very lucky and his future self (and *your* future self) will be especially glad that you did.

As I shared in the introduction, preteen and early teen boys have very specific, unique needs and conditions that must be met and put into place before they'll even consider reading for pleasure.

That's why this first book in the **Boys Will Read | Parent Series** is all about *your* preparation before you can help your son develop the reading habit (discussed in the second book in the series). I systematically take you through the steps necessary to develop your boy-responsive reading mindset and then to create the boy-responsive reading environment.

No special degrees or training are required. All you need is your commitment, time, and the space to expand *your* awareness and knowledge about preteen and early teen boys and their relationship to reading, before you interact with your son regarding *his* reading habit.

From start to finish, it should take about 30 days (more or less, depending on your schedule and prior knowledge) to read this book and complete the necessary action steps before you'll be ready and confident enough to work on your son's reading habit with him.

To help make the ideas, research and actions reader-friendly and doable for busy parents, I structured each building block in the book as follows:

- The What (The Building Blocks)
- The Why (The Ripple Effects)
- The How (The Action Steps)
- The Summary (The Key Takeaways)

The What (The Building Blocks)

Each building block is a specific action you must take before you can develop your son's reading habit. The building blocks are cumulative. Each one builds on the one(s) before it. To implement the ideas and actions in this book, it's important to read and implement each building block in the order they are given.

The first five blocks focus on you as a reader, and how you think about reading in *your* life. At first, it may feel uncomfortable to shift your current mindset to a boy-responsive reading mindset. You will need to remember your commitment and remember that it's a process that will result in positive changes for you and for your son. As I shared in the Introduction, there are no shortcuts, but this method does work!

You matter. Your beliefs, thoughts, words, actions and habits all shape what reading means for your son. By intentionally working through blocks 1–5, you will first re-shape your own thinking about reading, so that you can then help him do the same for himself.

Then it'll be time to wrap your head around creating the boy-responsive reading environment your son needs. Building blocks 6–10 show you exactly how to do it, so that, by the time you finish this book, you will be ready for the next book, which will show you how to instill the reading habit in your son.

Building Blocks 1–5: Developing the Boy-Responsive Reading Mindset

Believe
Invest
Read
Walk the Talk
Prioritize

Building Blocks 6–10: Creating the Boy-Responsive Reading Environment

Appreciate
Balance
Adjust
Pinpoint
Plan

The Why (The Ripple Effects)

This section shows you all the reasons *why* the building block you're reading about matters to your son.

I start each reason with the phrase, "Because you _____ (fill in the building block's name) … . After the ellipse, I demonstrate the positive present/future effects for your son when this need is met.

To further explain each specific reason, I use analogies, stories and examples from my own experience, coupled with pertinent research and information from books and resources that framed my thinking. By doing this, I'm providing you with the knowledge you'll need to frame your thinking for when you meet with your son.

The How (The Action Steps)

Each building block ends with a section of critical *action* steps for you to take. It's important to engage with and respond to *all* of the action steps, because this is when and how change occurs.

I created each action step to give you the opportunity to intentionally and thoughtfully *act* on what was learned in each Ripple Effects section, but that's not all.

Your completed action steps are not meant to be "once and done." You will need them again in Building Block 10, when you create your reading habit coach's **playbook**, to be used when you work with the second book in the series. Your responses to each action step are the foundation for your son's reading habit.

There are two ways you can keep track of your responses:

1. Put all of your answers in written form, either in a single notebook or by typing them into a computer, or

2. Print out the workbook I created for you and write your answers in that.

> Visit the link below to download the "Building Blocks Workbook."
>
> www.hillarytubin.com/freeworkbook

The Summary (The Key Takeaways)

Before moving on to the next building block, I will highlight important points to remember and carry forward while reading the rest of the book.

Now on to Building Block 1: Believe. This block is the foundation for everything that follows. Your beliefs set your thinking and willingness to act on the rest of the Building Blocks. Without the proper perspective, nothing else I share will make a difference. *With* a proper perspective, everything will make sense in terms of your overall goal of helping your son to develop his relationship to reading.

So let's get started with believing that your son will read!

❧ BUILDING BLOCK 1: BELIEVE ❧

Your son needs you to believe that he will read.

THE RIPPLE EFFECTS OF BELIEVING

Because you believe... you'll say YES to your son's future and so will he.

Your son needs to be prepared for something you can't see or touch or wrap your head around. To believe your son will read also means becoming informed and aware of what it will take for him to survive and successfully thrive in the future.

Here's a peek into what that will entail:

*"Adolescents entering the adult world in the 21st century will read and write more than at any other time in human history. They will need **advanced levels of literacy** to perform their jobs, run their households, act as citizens, and conduct their personal lives. They will need literacy to cope with the flood of information they will find everywhere they turn. They will need literacy to feed their imaginations so they can create the world of the future. In a complex and sometimes even dangerous world, their ability to read can be crucial."*—International Literacy Association[11]

The world is no longer just an industrial or service-based economy. When he graduates, your son will be expected to plunge right into a *global, knowledge-based economy*, one where human capital (expertise/know-how/skills of employees) is the currency. As I pointed out in the Introduction, right now the type of reading skills your son is expected to develop in school are not adequate. He needs to develop reading literacy, and that requires that reading for pleasure is added to his reading diet.

The way I see it, many high schools need to hand out time machines with their diplomas, because today's graduates are not being prepared for tomorrow. What they are being taught belongs to the past; it keeps them locked into a mindset that puts them at a disadvantage in the world they will actually occupy.

I'm not the only one who thinks this way.

In his book, *The Global Achievement Gap: Why Even Our Best Schools Don't Teach the New Survival Skills Our Children Need— And What We Can Do About It*, Tony Wagner shares the seven survival skills your son will need to acquire by his mid-20s in order to succeed. However, right now these are most likely not the ones he is being held accountable for in school. As you'll notice, literacy and self-learning underlies all seven skills.

Tony Wagner's Seven Survival Skills[12]

1. Critical thinking and problem-solving
2. Collaboration across networks and leading by influence
3. Agility and adaptability
4. Initiative and entrepreneurialism
5. Effective oral and written communication
6. Accessing and analyzing information
7. Curiosity and imagination

"In today's world, it's no longer how much you know that matters; it's what you can do with what you know... Life is not a multiple-choice test."—Tony Wagner

Awareness of what your son's "tomorrow" will require of him is key to *you* being able to help him prepare for it in ways that will bring him success. Understanding the role of strong literacy skills and self-learning is imperative. By believing that your son will read, you will readily open your mind to the value and importance of his developing the reading habit today, to prepare for his future success.

Because you believe... your son will gain the benefits that only the reading habit can give him.

As it turns out, cultivating the daily reading habit is the least expensive (libraries provide books for free), easiest, most effective, and advantageous way your son can shape his future for success, develop a competitive edge, and build his global, knowledge-based economy survival kit. He only needs 30 minutes every day to start the ball rolling, and to reap the cumulative effects of reading so that he thrives.

Below are the known researched benefits of having a daily reading habit:

- Higher all-around academic achievement and test scores[13]
- Strong reading skills, verbal cognitive (thinking) skills and cognitive stamina (mental effort)[14]
- More expansive background/general knowledge[15]
- More fully-developed vocabulary, essential for increased communication skills[16]
- Improved writing/spelling/language and math skills[17]
- More fully developed empathy, essential for improving people skills[18]
- More fully developed imagination and intellectual curiosity[19]
- Reduced stress[20]
- Reduced or delayed onset of Alzheimer's[21] and dementia[22]

Knowledge is power. The more you understand the benefits of reading, the more motivated you will be to help your son develop the reading habit. When you are motivated and understand how important it is for his future, you will communicate this importance, and that will act to break through his resistance to changing his present ways.

Because you believe... your son will feel safe and secure, enabling him to trust in what's possible.

It's important to be clear about the difference between *believing* your son will read and *hoping* your son will read, because only your act of *believing* will help your son feel safe and secure enough to do the work that is necessary for his future success.

When you believe something, you accept it as being true, even without proof. When you accept "My son will read" as being true, it becomes a real possibility. The image of him reading forms in your mind's eye, inspiring action and follow-through on your part. It is only when you believe that you act intentionally and purpose-fully towards making your belief become a reality. Consequently, if you *don't* see your son reading in your mind's eye, he won't. You must imagine it first, before it becomes real.

Hope, on the other hand, is to *want* something to be true but to do nothing to make it happen. It's not bad *per se* to hope that your son will read, but it does lack action, direction, a plan, urgency and agency—all the things your son needs from you to transform his non-reading habit into a reading habit. The "hope strategy" is more like crossing your fingers, throwing a penny in a fountain, or wishing upon a star that one day an outside force will arrive, make it happen, and poof, your son will read. Because hope is only *wishing*, it doesn't inspire you to act with intention, purpose or follow through.

Think of it like this:

When you *don't believe* your son will read, it's like you're standing outside the car, busy doing other things, while your son sits alone in the passenger seat, waiting and hoping that you see him there. The longer he waits for you to get behind the wheel to take him on his journey, the more he loses hope. Ultimately, he gives up on ever going anywhere. Sometimes somebody else volunteers to get behind the wheel and drive him, but not without a fight from your son. He's saving the seat for you. Eventually, he tires of waiting, gets out of the car, and moves onto something else.

When you *hope* your son will read, it's as if you're sitting in the back seat (behind the driver's seat), not ready to lead the way. Instead of taking the wheel yourself, you're waiting for someone else to drive the car. Meanwhile, your son is up front by himself, not sure who's in charge or who he can count on. All he knows is that—right now—it isn't you. Secretly, he hopes with all his might that you will move from the back seat to the driver's seat, sit beside him, and take control of the steering wheel, so his journey can begin.

When you *believe* your son will read, you're in the driver's seat, committing to take the wheel and lead the way. You're willing to own the responsibility and the pressure that comes with your son sitting next to you in the passenger seat. Feeling safe and secure is a big deal for him, but with you by his side, prepared and ready to go, your son trusts that anything is possible.

Here's why:

> "Your beliefs become your thoughts,
> Your thoughts become your words,
> Your words become your actions,
> Your actions become your habits,
> Your habits become your values,
> Your values become your destiny."
> —Mahatma Gandhi

Everything you think, say, do, and value stems from this belief. The first step is believing that your son will read and believing in your abilities to take him there. Then everything else follows.

Because you believe... your son will also believe.

Your son has no idea why he should read for 30 minutes every day. He has no idea that an investment in reading now will bring many times more rewards in his future. He has no idea what it means for him to become the best version of himself. What he needs is someone—just *one* person (but the more the better)—to believe that he deserves to reach his fullest potential and is willing to do what it takes to support him on his reading habit journey.

"A person must believe change is possible to successfully transform their habit."—Charles Duhigg

The challenge with believing change is possible is that belief doesn't emerge all by itself, and if it isn't firmly in place when things get tense, old habits reassert themselves quickly. To truly transform the habit, the odds for success go up tenfold within a community of support (even if the community is just one other person), because belief in change only emerges with the interactions and help of a group.

You need to become your son's supportive community of one. By believing he will read, you show your son how to believe in himself and his future. You show him what's possible, beyond what is comfortable for him now.

When you believe your son is capable of change, and that change is worth pursuing, he will also believe. You will lead him by your example.

ACTION STEPS

1. **Tough Question:** Do you believe it's possible your son will read for pleasure every day?

What I know from my experience is this: your thoughts, words, and actions about your son's reading habit all stem from your belief. Without this core belief in place as the foundation, the rest of the building blocks are a house of cards built on sand. So whether your answer is "Yes," "No," "Maybe," or "It depends on the day," by choosing to read this book, it shows that you have already taken the first step towards believing that your son will read.

2. Write a letter to your son

The purpose of writing a letter to your son is two-fold. First, writing things down brings clarity. The act of writing gives you the space and time to take what's swimming around in your head, focus your full attention on it, and explore its possibilities. Second, writing helps to take possibilities and turn them into concrete and verifiable reality. The act of writing and putting things down on paper makes you more committed to your goals and more likely to achieve success with them.

When you write a letter to your son, your words to him become a snapshot of how you see him—where he is today with his non-reading habit, and what you perceive about his interests, his desires for his future, and how he's going after them, etc. Your words will also help *you* become clear on why it's important to believe your son will read. Think of the letter as a contract with yourself, where you are committing to be the driver of your son's reading habit journey.

What do you write in the letter?

- It's important to date your letter, so you will know the exact moment you captured the snapshot. This will matter later.
- Describe the crossroads he is at right now. Be real and honest about your concerns, worry, love and belief in him. Let him know how you're planning to help and support him (as the driver) and how he'll be able to count on you. Use the information in the Introduction and in this building block to help frame your letter and what you might want to share with him. The more you express to your son, the more committed you'll become.
- When you finish writing this letter, put it away until Building Block 10, when it will become part of your reading habit playbook.

KEY TAKEAWAYS... Building Block 1: Believe

- Your son needs a community of at least one to believe in him, so he will believe in himself.
- Your son needs you in the driver's seat on his reading habit journey, so he can feel safe and secure enough to trust that anything's possible.
- A global, knowledge-based economy requires strong literacy skills for success and survival. Your son needs you to believe that he *will* read and say YES to his future success.

- The researched benefits of the daily reading habit are truly amazing. By believing that your son will read, you make it possible for him to take advantage of what the reading habit has to offer.

Once you believe, you'll be ready to invest in your own reading life. This moment is like when the flight attendant reminds you to take care of your oxygen mask before you help your children put on their masks.

Get ready to put on your oxygen mask in Building Block 2: Invest.

Visit the link below to learn my story of how I moved from the backseat into the driver's seat for the reading habit journey.

> I created this pdf for you to share what I went through, warts and all, when I first tried to help boys read for pleasure. It's meant to encourage, inspire and show you what's possible when you believe that boys will read.
>
> http://www.hillarytubin.com/freemystorypdf

✕ BUILDING BLOCK 2: INVEST ✕

Your son needs you to invest in your own reading habit before investing in his.

THE RIPPLE EFFECTS OF INVESTING

Because you invest... you'll have *skin in the reading game* and so will your son.

Committing to take the wheel and sit in the driver's seat is both an act of love—because you want the best for your son and his future—and grit. Yes, grit. From here on out, love for your son underlies each building block, but it's your sense of purpose, determination and resolve that will keep you driving, even when you want to stop, hop in the back seat or get out of the car.

That's why it's imperative that you first believe that your son will read. This belief opens up your heart to something bigger than yourself. It inspires you to think purposefully, take action and do what is necessary, even when what's necessary is uncomfortable or difficult for you.

Now it's time to take your belief one step further.

For your son to successfully transform his non-reading habit into the reading habit, he needs to know you have "skin in the reading game" and are willing to expose yourself to the same risk you're asking of him.

But what exactly do I mean when I say "skin in the reading game"?

"Skin in the reading game" means:

1. Making a personal investment in your own reading, so you can discuss with your son the costs and benefits of including the daily reading habit in *his* day from the perspective of personal experience.
2. Stretching, putting yourself out there, feeling uncomfortable and paying a cost in terms of your schedule, before expecting your son to do the same with *his* reading.

Without skin in the reading game, your son will think it's unfair to expect him to do something you don't or won't do, no matter how good for him it might be. It's easy to tell him why he *should* be reading, but without shouldering the challenges that come along with this type of transformation, your words will mean very little. You need to lead by example—in this case, your example of having a reading habit of your own.

What you want is to show him **credible commitment**. With this type of commitment, you'll be able to honestly share with your son why he should invest in his reading habit and show him how to find the grit to do so. Through first-hand experience, you'll understand that transforming is tough, mistakes are made, and derailment happens, but you'll also be able to inspire, influence and mentor him toward success, because you did it yourself.

Skin in the reading game means you have more than love for your son and belief in his future; it means you have the mettle it takes to expose yourself to and invest in your own reading, and to be part of the solution.

Because you invest... you'll be able to help your son re-define the word *reading*.

For you to re-define the word reading for yourself (and later for your son), you must first deal with two reading habit myths. These myths are what I call the non-reading habit mindset. The parents of the boys who were unable/unwilling to utilize the 10 Building Blocks typically came to the table with these two myths in place. The parents of the boys who developed a reading habit had what I call the reading mindset; they understood that reading is greater than the sum of its individual parts.

Myth: Non-Reading Mindset	Big Picture: Reading Mindset
People are born with an innate talent, gift, or intelligence for enjoying reading that can't be taught. Someone either has the "reading for pleasure" gene or they don't; this is set in stone and unchangeable.	Readers are made, not born. The reading habit can be taught through modeling and deliberate design. Everyone has the capacity to read for pleasure when the right reading mindset, support and environment are in place.
Reading is only a skill, which can be broken down into its parts (decoding, fluency, comprehension) and mandated by someone else to be done in the form of school work, homework or as part of paid work.	Understands that reading is a skill, but sees reading as so much more. Reading provides the opportunity to self-learn based on interests, and daily reading for pleasure is an enjoyable, beneficial, desirable and healthy life habit to be cultivated.

Let's look more closely at the differences between a boy with the *non-reading* mindset and a boy with the *reading* mindset.

Non-reading mindset: This boy believes he's not a reader and will never be a reader. No one in his family reads for pleasure, and they say it's because it's not in their DNA. To him, reading often means decoding words and skimming so he can get the answers right to multiple-choice comprehension questions. He doesn't pursue interests that require him to read.

Reading mindset: This boy didn't always love to read, but his mom showed him that reading can be fun and enjoyable. She helped him transform his non-reading habit, and every night before going to bed, he started reading about things he loves. Now he can't fall asleep without learning something new.

Can you see the two different mindsets at play here? The non-reading mindset limits reading's possibilities in the boy's life because he believes the myths, he sees the example set by those around him, and he can't shift his mindset on his own. This boy needs someone to show him how to re-define reading, and that re-definition must begin by untangling the catch-all word, "reading."

Teachers, parents, the media, the government—basically every-one—labels anything that is *reading-related* as "reading," without any distinctions, descriptors or purpose attached. Unfortunately, boys can't differentiate one type of reading experience from another on their own, so they lump together everything that is reading-related and follow the example set by the adults around them.

I call that action of lumping everything together under the single word, "reading," a tangled, hot mess. "Tangled," as in a big, nasty, impossible knot where things that shouldn't be connected are, and "hot mess" because of Freud's "pleasure-pain principle," that states people are motivated to approach pleasurable things and avoid painful things.

The instant the boys I taught heard the word "reading," I witnessed the pleasure-pain principle over and over and over again. They never said it, but "avoid pain, avoid pain, avoid pain" was written all over their faces, in their eyes, their behaviors, and—most telling—their shudders of disbelief when I put the word pleasure together with the word reading. To them, nothing about reading equaled their definition of pleasure, but it did equal pain, so it needed to be avoided at all costs. I share actual examples of this pain avoidance in Building Block 6: Appreciation.

For now, I want to share what I discovered through actual conversations with boys. I heard similar stories time and again. A pattern emerged. Aliterate boys always shared at least one painful reading experience they had had in the past and kept hidden, or— if they did share—they thought no one really cared.

Instead, they stuffed their reading pain deep down, where it got all tangled up into an impossible knot. This emotional stuffing then shut out any possibility of reading for pleasure (and all of its benefits) from their lives. It essentially created the oil and water effect I talked about in the Introduction. These boys had an active aversion to reading because for them, it was directly associated with pain.

I knew it was up to me to help boys re-define the word "reading," but first I needed to become crystal clear on the types of reading they viewed as pain, then give each type a name and a valid purpose for doing it that made sense to preteen and early teen boys. Here's what I created:

Type of Reading	Purpose	Examples	Boys' Views
Foundational	Critical to crack the code and understand what's written on the page; all other reading is built on this type; it is essential for reading success.	Reading skills/ fluency/ decoding/ phonics Reading comprehension/ strategies/ questions	Pain
Standardized	Compares readers to proficiency standards and the norm; accountability; used as a gatekeeper to goals and advancement (driver's license; SATs, LSATs, GREs, work certifications for jobs/ promotions/raises, etc.)	Reading test prep: short texts, worksheets/work to practice Reading standardized tests: short texts with multiple-choice questions and/or essays; high-stakes	Pain
Mandatory	Important to understand and do to successfully survive in the world of school, work and duty (household, as a citizen, etc.)	Reading for someone else: school work, homework, or forced-on-them reading material that's "boring, stupid or uninteresting."	Pain
Pleasure	Critical to successfully thrive in school, work and the world.	Reading for oneself: for fun, to learn, to grow, to be entertained	Boys avoid at all costs because they believe it's optional

It's tough for boys and reading for pleasure to mix because, most likely, the focus has been on foundational, standardized and/or mandatory reading—the pain-inducing types—since they turned

9 years old. At home, you probably focus on these three types of reading, too, because as your son's parent, his success in school matters to you.

In moderation and with purpose, reading skills, reading comprehension, reading test prep, reading testing, and reading for someone else are important and have value for your son. However, for most boys, school reading hasn't been moderated, presented to them purposefully, or in a boy-responsive way. Until the reading "hot mess" is untangled in his mind, your son will continue to equate *all* reading with pain.

When I started to communicate with boys and used the terms above, it opened the door to re-defining reading. Instead of calling everything "reading," I made sure to distinguish between the four types and their purpose whenever I talked/taught reading. This act alone untangled the biggest, tightest knot and cleaned up the hot mess. As soon as boys stopped equating *all* reading with pain and understood the four purposes of reading, a space opened up for pleasure reading to exist, too.

Re-defining reading for your son means becoming aware of the types of reading that typically cause boys pain. Because you invest and have skin in the game, this new awareness will drive you forward to figure out what may be causing your son's reading pain, plus you'll apply what you learned about the pleasure/pain principle in your own reading life, as well.

Because you invest... you'll understand why pleasure reading at home (not just school reading) matters for your son's future success.

Do you know the one trait that great male business and world leaders and billionaires have in common? I mean the likes of Phil Knight from Nike, Dee Hock (the founder of Visa), Elon Musk (founder of PayPal), Bill Gates, Steve Jobs, Warren Buffet, Mark Zuckerberg, and Presidents Obama, Clinton and Bush. Besides having power and money, they all are avid readers. These very busy men read all the time.

Reading shaped them into who they are, starting when they were young, and continues to shape them today.

That's why, in his article, "For Those Who Want to Lead, Read," John Coleman is also concerned about the lack of reading right now in the United States. He explains that great leaders (such as the men mentioned above) read to expand how they think and to cultivate knowledge, habits and talents to improve themselves and their organizations. Engaged reading (which is what he calls reading for pleasure) is what fuels the insight, innovation, empathy, and personal effectiveness necessary to lead, and—without this habit in place—there is no other substitute for gaining these skills.[23]

Recent research on reading actually shows that one of the best ways to practice and improve empathy and social skills is by reading fiction. In her article, "The Business Case for Reading Novels," Anne Kreamer shared that, to be successful in business today, it's important to "interpret and respond to those different from us—colleagues, employees, bosses, customers, and clients— particularly in a globalized economy."

Because reading fiction creates a lived-through experience, it gives readers the time and opportunity to practice thinking about other people's feelings, emotions, and points of view. They then can carry over this empathy practice—this exercising of emotions—into their real lives, when interacting with people face-to-face or through email or on calls. When they do, it makes a huge difference in their work life. Not only will they have a better perspective and understanding of the people around them, a study found that people who were rated highest by their peers in emotional intelligence (empathy) also received bigger raises and were promoted more frequently.[24]

Empathy is practiced by reading fiction. Think how far ahead your son will be (as compared to non-readers) in developing his emotional intelligence if he starts reading now. Think about where you might find *yourself* if you start investing in your own reading habit, too. In addition, having empathy also means that relationships with others (family, friends, colleagues, bosses, significant others) will benefit, as well.[25]

Reading nonfiction is also valuable to future success.

In his article, "16 Rich Habits," Tom Corley shares what he uncovered after years of researching the daily habits of financially-successful adults, compared to financially-struggling adults. There were definite differences between the two groups, but those differences weren't circumstance, genetics, talent, intelligence or personality. Instead, it's all about one's mindset and what's valued, prioritized and practiced each and every day. The best news is that everyone has access to these habits, and two of the most important daily habits practiced by financially-successful adults are reading every day and limiting television watching and internet browsing.

Mr. Corley found that 88% of wealthy people read for 30 minutes or more a day. They mostly read nonfiction (current events, educational career-related material, biographies of successful people, personal development, and history) to improve themselves and gain a competitive edge. They also read to increase their knowledge and open their eyes to more opportunities, because with opportunity comes the potential for more wealth.[26]

School reading is mandatory and something everyone receives. It's your son's *home* reading that will put him on track for his future success.

Because you invest... you'll unpack your reading story to help your son create his new reading story.

In this book, my focus is squarely on reading for pleasure and helping you to help your son cultivate the reading habit for his present and future success. However, without asking you to dig deep into the other three types of reading in your own life, it just won't happen.

Past experiences shape the present, and reading is no different. Even though it is a subject in school, reading brings with it much more baggage than one would expect. Most adults don't realize the pained faces they make when the word "reading" comes up or the comments rolling off their tongue or the non-verbal body language they display.

My boys were the ones who told me about this. I didn't see it or believe them until I unpacked my own relationship with reading. Then I started to notice all the different signals parents gave off when I talked to them about reading: arms crossed, blank stares, pain in their eyes, pushing the chair back away from the table, sighing, grunting, frowning, shaking their head, arguing, smiling, leaning forward, and saying "thank you," to name a few.

Your son notices *your* body language and micro-expressions when *you* talk about reading. Depending on what they are, they may add to his pain without you even knowing that that's what's going on for him. How you see yourself as a reader, what you value and believe about reading books for pleasure—not what you say— impacts how your son sees himself as a reader and whether he values reading. This is because you and your son have an inter-twined reading history, starting from when he was born.

Based on your past experiences with reading, when your son was an infant, toddler, preschooler, and kindergartner, you either read aloud every day or you didn't. Those same experiences also influ-enced whether you routinely went to the library and/or bookstore with your son, and how you talked about reading when you were around him. The reading decisions you made back then were the start of your intertwined reading history with your son, and it continues today, consciously or not.

My mom and dad both read every day while I was growing up, and when I was little, my mom took me to the library. That's because *her* mom and dad read and took her to the library. I became an avid reader, which made all the difference in my life—by chance, not by intention—only because this was how things were done in my family from one generation to the next. Math, on the other hand, was another story. I grew up pre-STEM, and I desperately needed one girl-responsive adult to help me relate well to math. It took until my 40s to finally find the person who did that for me.

Your son doesn't have to wait until he's an adult to re-define reading. By unpacking your reading story and shining a light on it, you'll be able to make a difference right now. Because you invest, your son will see you shift your attitude and your mindset about reading, and then he'll do the same, following your example.

"The best time to plant a tree was 20 years ago. The second best time is now."—Chinese Proverb

ACTION STEPS

1. Tough Question: Do you invest in your own reading habit?

Even if you don't or you haven't in a while, this building block is all about priming the pump for what comes next. It's meant to shake things up and get you thinking about your reading life more consciously. By reflecting on this, you'll start to make intentional changes to help your son, because if you don't, you'll be leaving his reading habit to chance.

2. Unpack Your Reading Stories

Believing your son will read opens up the door for you to have skin in the reading game. When you have skin in the reading game, you're also willing to risk exposure and unpack your relationship with reading, even if it is uncomfortable. It's actually the cost of your discomfort and the exposure to risk that makes the unpacking process a critical and powerful action step.

By reflecting on your past reading experiences (and your son's, too), you move closer to seeing how the different types of reading played/are playing out in your intertwined reading lives. From there, re-defining reading becomes possible.

To help you think about your reading experiences with the four types of reading, I have provided descriptions and questions to get your memories flowing. It's okay if you can't remember everything; just jot down as much as you can. It's the process of looking backwards to move forwards that gives you skin in the reading game, not how many questions you can answer about reading when you are writing in your notebook or the workbook.

The Four Types of Reading and Their Influence on Your Life

Foundational

- ## Reading skills/fluency/decoding/phonics

I found many boys' most painful stories started here. They equated reading when they were younger to mean sitting perfectly still when they needed to stand or move, having to sound things out slowly instead of words popping in their heads instantly, and being expected to read out loud fluently like the girls did, when they knew they couldn't.

In their minds, all components of learning how to read were anti- what they were good at and enjoyed about life—being active/ physical, getting dirty, making a mess, playing, building, doing things fast and doing what's easy. For many, "breaking the code" didn't happen as expected, and they had to keep doing more phonics and fluency work at school and home. Boys shared with me the pressure they felt and thought they didn't measure up as a reader, even though they had tried their best.

It's important for you to understand how this type of reading played out in your childhood to gain a better sense of how you may have unconsciously played this out in your son's life.

- When did you learn to read?
- Did you learn quickly and easily or do you remember strug- gling to "break the code"?
- How did the people around you respond to your reading skills? Praise? Criticism? Both?

- In your mind, do you remember seeing school and home reading as the same or different? Did your parents read aloud to you or re-enforce how reading skills were taught in school?
- How did you help your son learn how to read? The same as or different from you? Did you read aloud to him or reinforce what happened in school?

- **Reading comprehension/strategies/questions**

Once reading skills are in place, or even if they're not, by third grade boys are expected to understand what they're reading, even if they hate what they're reading. This comes in the form of learning strategies like envisioning, predicting, connecting and inferring, and being asked a lot of questions at the end of a story. For many boys, this feels like an inquisition, especially since many still don't read as fast or as fluently as girls. If they didn't equate type 1 (foundational) with pain, many begin to equate type 2 (comprehension/strategies/questions) that way.

- What are your memories about reading in school? Did your teachers read aloud every day for at least 15 minutes to your class and use real books to teach, or did you read from a basal/anthology book and fill in workbook pages?
- Did you sit still during reading and raise your hand to answer questions the teacher asked, or were you able to authentically respond to books?
- How did your school experience with comprehension make you feel about reading?
- What is your son's experience with comprehension in school? How do you think it makes him feel about reading?

Standardized

- ## Reading test prep

As your son moves up through the grades, reading test prep becomes the norm. Depending on his school, he is spending much of his time reading short stories and answering multiple-choice questions to practice for the high-stakes test in March or April. Test prep reading only helps with one thing—getting better at taking tests. It can't be extrapolated and used to develop readers of books.

- How much reading test prep did you do while you were in elementary and middle school? As much as your son, more or less?
- If your school reading experience included test prep, how did it impact your feelings towards reading? If you didn't have much experience with test prep, how do you think it would impact your feelings towards reading?
- What is your son's experience with reading test prep in school? How do you think it makes him feel about reading?

- ## Reading standardized tests/multiple-choice questions/ high-stakes

Standardized tests have their usefulness, but in today's educational climate, your son will take six high-stakes standardized tests that measure who he is as a reader before he takes his driver's permit test and the SATs. Not only does your son have his own understanding of who he is as a reader but, starting in third grade, he is also given a label: advanced, proficient, basic or below basic. He has no idea what these terms mean except advanced is the best, proficient means good enough, and basic and below basic mean more test prep and practice because he's not good enough. Nobody helps boys to make sense of these four labels and to use this knowledge to improve their reading. Consequently, boys make up their own interpretations and, without outside help, their interpretations can be dangerous to their reading lives.

- What role did standardized tests play in your reading life? How much impact did they have on how you saw yourself as a reader?
- Did you love taking these types of tests or did they cause you fear and anxiety? Where did you usually fall on the bell-shaped curve (top, average, below average)?
- Do you take standardized tests today for work certifications, etc.? How do you feel about them as an adult?
- How has your son done on the reading standardized tests he's taken so far? Do you understand what his scores tell you about how he uses his mind while he reads?
- How do you talk to your son about standardized tests and his results, and how do you think this impacts his reading life? What do you think *he* thinks his scores mean?

Mandatory

- **Reading for someone else/school work/homework**

Having a choice about what they read is a huge issue for boys, which is why mandatory reading kills it for them. For them, being forced to read is a fate worse than death, and their negative feelings about someone else's choices override everything. They just can't get beyond how much they hate a certain book to see the forest through the trees. Because most of the books they read for school are mandatory, this attitude toward reading snowballs, and they are trapped in a downward spiral that worsens over time.

- Looking back on your school career, how did you feel about the mandatory reading thrust upon you? Describe some of the books you loved and some that you hated. What made the difference? A teacher? The content? Prior knowledge on the topic? Interest?
- Did your parents make you read certain books or disapprove of what you enjoyed reading? How did that make you feel?
- How do you feel about mandatory reading in your life as an adult? Work reading? Duty reading like mortgage agreements or understanding your insurance policy terms and conditions? What happens to you if you don't read your mandatory reading?
- How does your son feel about mandatory reading in his life? How do you help him navigate all of his reading homework, whether it's for his English, social studies or science class?
- Do you want your son to read books that he's not interested in reading? How do you suggest these books to him? Do you think he sees them as suggestions or being forced on him? Why might this matter?

Pleasure

- **Reading for oneself/fun/entertainment/to grow/to learn**

This type of reading is not: 1) a skill; 2) followed by a set of questions to check one's understanding or a standardized multiple-choice test; or 3) forced upon you. This type of reading is a positive, beneficial and healthy habit that hopefully happens every day. As a person, you grow in leaps and bounds, so you can become the best version of yourself. It happens during your spare time because you *want it to*, because you value it in your life. Boys who were read to aloud when they were little consistently viewed this time as a special and pleasurable reading experience. Once it ended for them, they no longer equated reading with pleasure.

- What types of things did you love to read? Did your parents support and appreciate what you read?
- Were your parents readers when you were growing up? How do you know? What about other family members? Your friends?
- How does reading for pleasure fit into your life today?
- Does your son think you read for pleasure? How do you think he formed his opinion?
- Were you read aloud to when you were little? Did you read aloud to your son? If yes, how old was he when you stopped? Did he ask you to stop or did you stop because he was in school?

Add anything else about your past reading history or your son's present reading history that you think is important. As you read through this book, other memories may surface. Please keep adding these other stories about your reading life to this section. Make sure to identify the type of reading it was, to keep sorting out what kinds of reading were pleasurable for you and which ones weren't. This will enable you to begin to re-frame your relationship to reading and to more clearly understand your son's relationship to reading, too.

KEY TAKEAWAYS… Building Block 2: Invest

- Having skin in the reading game makes you more credible in your son's eyes; it shows him that you're in this together.
- Everything related to reading is called *reading*, without any distinctions, descriptors or purpose attached. There are actually four types of reading: foundational, standardized, mandatory, and pleasure, and each means something different. Unfor-

tunately, they get tangled together in boys' minds, and they associate all reading with pain, including reading for pleasure.
- Leaders and wealthy people read for pleasure every day because they know it gives them a competitive advantage.
- Your past experiences with reading shape how you share reading with your son, verbally and non-verbally. By unpacking your reading stories, and understanding your own feelings toward reading, you can begin to re-define reading for your son.

Now that you have invested in your reading habit and have skin in the reading game, it's time to include reading for pleasure into your life. Building Block 3: Read will help you to understand why you must become a reading role model for your son and how to start to include reading into your life.

Visit the link below to download the "Turn Off to Tune In" exercise I created for you.

The "Turn Off to Tune In" exercise will help you to breathe and keep your head clear while answering the questions for Action Step 2, Unpacking Your Reading Story. Additionally, it is a great technique to use to keep you calm when talking to your son about reading.

http://www.hillarytubin.com/freeturnoffexercise

✦ BUILDING BLOCK 3: READ ✦

Your son needs you to be his reading role model.

THE RIPPLE EFFECTS OF READING

Because *you* read... your son will have the reading role model he needs, in order for *him* to read.

Football is one example of an activity with lots of visibility and multiple opportunities for your son to see modeling. He probably has watched lots of football games on television or in real life (professional, college, high school, in his neighborhood). In addition to your son *seeing* football players, people also talk about football. Before the game, they make predictions about what is going to happen, depending on the teams playing. During the game, there's debate, thinking and evaluation of what just happened and what might happen next. After the game is over, further comments are shared on television, over the radio, in the newspaper and between family members, friends, colleagues and even strangers.

This level of visual and verbal exposure helps your son immensely. If he plays football or wants to play football, there are plenty of models available to guide him and to help him understand what to expect in a football game. Now he needs *you* to show him what to expect in the reading game.

If you're a female, you might be wondering whether your son needs a male reading role model, in order to make a difference in his reading life. It's a very important question to explore. Being female, I also wondered and worried if my modeling was enough.

Over time I learned yes, yes it was, as long as I approached it with a boy-responsive mindset and as if I were a sports coach.

Being a boy-responsive female reading role model means that you understand that you read differently and for different purposes than your son does or will. By recognizing and embracing those differences, your modeling becomes increasingly more effective and influential in opening him up to reading. It's also critical to value the role of adult *male* readers in your son's life, by making sure he has opportunities to see and interact with men reading for pleasure.

Your son's male reading role models can be his dad, brother, cousin, coach, teacher, uncle, neighbor, or best friend's dad. He can connect with them face-to-face, on Skype/FaceTime, through email, texts, or by phone. Because you will be your son's *primary* reading role model, interaction doesn't need to happen all the time with the same adult male reader; think of it as an essential supplement.

If you're a male reading this book, make sure your son also has female reading role models to enrich his reading life. The more models the better!

Because you read… research shows that your son will read.

In their *2015 Kids & Family Reading Report,* Scholastic found there are three powerful predictors that tell you whether your son will be a frequent reader.[27]

Powerful Predictors: 9- to 14-year-olds	• He has parents who are frequent readers. • He strongly believes reading for fun is important. • He rates himself as highly enjoying reading.
Additional Predictors: 9- to 11-year-olds	• He was frequently read to aloud before kindergarten and is currently being read to aloud at home. • His parents allow him to choose books that let him use his imagination. • His time online is balanced with reading and other activities.
Additional Predictors: 12- to 14-year-olds	• He will read more books after being introduced to e-books. • His parents encourage reading for pleasure and help him to find books he will like. • His parents encourage reading by putting limits on his screen time, build reading into his schedule, and reads the same book as he does, so they can talk about it together. • He lives in a house with more than one hundred books.

The above predictors are important food for thought regarding your current reading habit. When *you* read for pleasure, you model reading for your son as an enjoyable, important activity that is worth spending time doing, even when the computer or television beckons. It also makes it more likely that you will encourage your son to read, engage with him around books, and help him choose books that he might enjoy.

Without *your* modeling what being a reader looks like, sounds like, and feels like for your son, he won't know where to begin or how to have skin in *his* reading game. Otherwise, it will be "out of sight, out of mind." When he doesn't actually see people read, for him it means it doesn't happen. How can it be otherwise?

In her book, *The Smartest Kids in the World: And How They Got That Way,* Amanda Ripley confirms Scholastic's 2015 report and the importance of parents modeling reading and talking about books. She dug deep into the results of the 2009 PISA test (administered to 15-year olds around the globe) because she was very curious to learn how the smartest kids in reading and math got to be that way. One important finding she discovered stated that **parents and home environments** dramatically impact reading scores, even more than educational policy.[28]

Below are three of the **global parenting patterns** that produce the **high reading scores** that policy can't dictate:

- Kids whose parents read aloud to them when they were little did much better in reading across the globe.
- Kids whose parents discussed movies, books and current events with them did better in reading, and when parents talked to their kids about complicated social issues, they also enjoyed reading more.
- Kids whose parents read for pleasure at home, also enjoyed reading for pleasure. This stayed constant across countries and family income.[29]

"Kids could see what parents valued, and it mattered more than what parents said."—Amanda Ripley

When your son sees *you* read, he'll know it's something important for him to consider as valuable.

Because you read... you'll expand your knowledge and gain the benefits reading offers, too.

Let's say someone only eats junk food, drinks soda, and gets five hours of sleep a night, but they still function in their life, go to work and get a paycheck. Do you think this person can grasp how much more productive they'd be and energetic they'd feel if they started eating healthy, drinking water, and added a few hours more of sleep to their life?

Probably not. Because without a reference point, the benefits of a healthy lifestyle won't seem real, plausible or worth the trouble. Until fruits, vegetables, water and sleep become a consistent part of someone's life, it's impossible for them to imagine the vast differences in mental acuity and physical well-being that result, according to which of the two lifestyles one follows.

Including the reading habit into your life is similar. Unless you were once a reader who has since stopped reading, you won't be able to imagine what you've been missing.

When you commit to be in the driver's seat for your son's reading habit, it also means you're committing to develop yourself as a reader; the one won't happen without the other. In addition to helping your son, reading might even bring *you* new and unexpected opportunities.

In his article, "5 Ways Reading Makes You A Better Leader: The Science Behind Reading and Influence," Michael Hyatt (former CEO and author of bestselling leadership books), shares how people who *do* read can turn the decline of reading in America into an opportunity and advantage in business and political environments. The way Hyatt sees it, "a readership crisis is really a leadership crisis." He's a reader, and he knows very few leaders who aren't also readers. With fewer people reading, it will most likely be the readers who position themselves to stand out in the marketplace and be equipped to move into leadership types of roles.[30]

The five ways Hyatt feels reading can "uniquely develop and empower leaders" are very similar to the researched benefits I shared in Building Block 1: Believe. They are:

1. Reading makes us better thinkers (improves judgment, increases problem-solving abilities).

2. Reading improves our people skills (exercises empathy and ability to understand and relate to people, increases emotional IQ).

3. Reading helps us master communication (expands vocabulary and ability to choose better words in speaking and writing).

4. Reading helps us relax (lowers stress levels in as few as six minutes, stimulates creativity and engages imagination).

5. Reading keeps us young (the best way to stay mentally sharp through the aging process).[31]

Maybe you aren't interested in growing or gaining influence or being in a leadership role at work, but think about how reading can also improve your day-to-day life. It's definitely a habit worth pursuing and doing together with your son. When both of you read, you'll understand each other better, communicate better and be less stressed.

How amazing does *that* sound?

Over the years, I have watched parents and their sons who read together grow and deepen their relationship. Because of their shared reading habit, they started to talk more and share more about what they were learning and enjoying, and how it mattered to them. These conversations around books also allowed them to discuss tough topics and problem-solve them in an open, non-threatening and honest way.

Books are powerful tools of communication. When *you* read, you'll want to engage more with your son because you'll start to notice things that he might enjoy or be interested in. Sharing your knowledge, hopes, and dreams with your son opens doors for both of you, instead of closing them. I found preteen and early teen boys like nothing more than hearing you say, "When I was reading this really cool book/article about _____ , I thought of you."

Without you yourself reading, you lose out on an opportunity to get to know your son better and for him to get to know you better, which—to me—is the greatest benefit of all.

ACTION STEPS

1. Tough Question: Do you read every day where your son can see you doing that?

To transform your son's *non-reading habit* into his *reading habit* means that you need to do more than just read. Even though that's a fantastic starting place, you need to read where he can see you reading. This act of public reading shows your son that you value reading. Remember, he only knows what you model for him. If you're not reading where he can see you, in his mind you don't actually read, and therefore you don't value reading.

2. Read at least five days a week.

- Find books you want to read (this one is a great place to start!). Go to the library. Check out Amazon's Kindle Store for e-books and audiobooks. Ask friends and family for recommendations. Read the newspaper or a magazine. Find books about a hobby or an interest. Join a book club or start one for support. Check out the books in the Further Reading list I created for you (the link is at the end of the chapter).

- Determine where you want to read and what time of day works best for you to read in front of your son (at the kitchen table in the morning, on the couch in the afternoon or evening, listen to an audiobook in the car, or go to bed to read instead of watching TV).
- Let your family know ahead of time that you're adding reading to your life, and that you'll be off limits for 5–10 minutes every day and can't be disturbed. Lay out the expectations for your reading time and why they're important to you.
- At least five days a week, read where your son can see you engaged with a book or reading material or when he knows you're engaged with a book. Enjoy yourself. Smile. Pretend to read at first, if you have to. Pretend to enjoy reading, if you have to.
- Sprinkle what you're reading into conversations with your son, family and friends. Talk positively about what you read and make sure to differentiate the reasons you're reading (standardized, mandatory or pleasure).

3. Brainstorm a list of possible adult male reading role models for your son (or—if you're a male—adult *female* reading role models).

On *my* list, I included the males in the school building, and I also figured out ways to bring in as many male readers as possible. My grandfather read aloud, and dads/older brothers and older male students participated in book clubs, met one-on-one or also read aloud. During parent's night and parent/teacher conferences, I chatted with the dads who were there about the importance of reading *anything* in front of their sons (the newspaper, work documents, a lease agreement, etc.) and to talk about the purpose of the reading in a positive way. I also encouraged dads to have a book club with their son and to include other males (adults or son's friends), too.

- In a notebook or the workbook, brainstorm a list of all the adult males in your son's life (more is better). Put a checkmark next to the males whom you know are also readers. If you're not sure, put a question mark next to the name, and if you know for a fact they don't read, put a circle next to the name.
- Now make a star next to the males you know your son looks up to. It doesn't matter if he has a question mark or circle next to his name; still make a star next to his name.
- Write a new list that contains the names with a star. Read each name and think about whether this person might be willing and interested in being an adult male reading role model for your son (even if they don't read). Write down "yes," "maybe," or "no," and why you think this may be true (too busy, loves your son and will do anything to help, different time zone, no access, hates to read...).
- Using what you've learned so far in this book, jot down a few notes to yourself about how you might approach the "yes" group, the "maybe" group, and the "no" group to enlist their support in helping you help your son transform his non-reading habit into his reading habit. Make sure to explain 1) what you're doing and why; 2) your role, and how you would love them to become a reading role model for your son; 3) why it's important for your son; and 4) how you see them becoming involved.
- Contact the people on the list (face-to-face, phone call or email works best), starting with the "no" group first, then the "maybe" group, and ending with the "yes" group. It's important to start with the "no" group because they might surprise you. What I found with this group of adult males was that many of

them wanted to start reading themselves, but didn't have the motivation or inspiration to do so. When they knew it would help change the future trajectory for boys, they stepped up for it, big time!

- Once someone says "yes," ask them how much they want to be involved and create an action plan with them. Each one can contribute in whatever way they feel comfortable (it could be just a check-in to ask your son what he's reading, recommending books, talking about books, doing a book club together, going on a road trip and researching beforehand, etc.). Remember, you're the primary role model and they are the essential supplements.
- Finalize your list. If necessary, go back to your original brainstorm list and enlist the help of those people.

KEY TAKEAWAYS... Building Block 3: Read

- Without at least one primary reading role model, your son will not know how to participate in the reading game and what is expected of him as a reader.
- Research finds that if parents frequently read for pleasure, their children will enjoy reading and read for pleasure, too. Research also finds that when parents intentionally encourage early teen boys to read, recommend books for them to read, and discuss books and complicated social issues with them, they are more likely to read.
- By becoming your son's reading role model, you'll expand your own knowledge and gain the benefits of reading, too.

When you start to read in front of your son, you're ready to move to Building Block 4: Walk the Talk. Because without first doing the reading walk, your son won't care to hear your reading talk.

Visit the link below to download the Resources and Further Reading list of books I created for you.

You will find books I highly recommend that complement and enrich each Building Block. I've read every book on the list and each one framed my thinking about boys and books in a profound way throughout my journey. My hope is that the books I suggest might do the same for you.

http://www.hillarytubin.com/freefurtherreadinglist

✤ BUILDING BLOCK 4: WALK THE TALK ✤

Your son needs to trust that you are walking the reading talk
(the credibility factor).

THE RIPPLE EFFECTS OF WALKING THE TALK

**Because you walk the talk... your son will see you as a
credible reading resource.**

Boys expect their parents—and all adults, for that matter—to walk
their talk and practice what they preach, especially when it comes
to reading. Because reading causes them pain, boys pay close
attention to your every move, even when they seem like they're
doing something else. Typically, adults think it's the girls who are
paying attention (and they do), but girls are not like boys regarding
reading.

Really, it's true, and it's one of the many reasons that I only focus
on boys in this series of books. Throughout my years of observing
and talking with preteen and early teen boys, once they had the
words to share their feelings, I was surprised by how much they
noticed and felt things. Because of their non-reading habit, many
boys lacked the vocabulary of emotions that one gains through
reading books. Instead, they stewed about adults not having skin
in the reading game and, even more so, they became downright
angry when they felt adults told them one thing about reading and
did another themselves—the "Do as I say, not do as I do" syndrome.

From my conversations with boys, I learned there is only one way of walking the reading talk that makes adults credible in their eyes. To explain this, I created a chart with different Walk the Talk combinations. The Walk column lists the ways you might *show* your son your reading habit, and the Talk column lists the types of things you might *say* to your son about reading.

The goal is to find the combination where the reading action and the reading words are congruent. When the combination hits the mark, trust me, you'll know, and this is the message your son wants and expects from you.

Try to match up the first box in the Walk column with each of the boxes in the Talk column. Then move to the second box in the Walk column and repeat. Then the third box and fourth box. Pay attention to which combination *feels* like a credible reading resource to you.

Walk	Talk
I read books/other reading material (newspapers, work material, important mail) in front of my son every day.	I talk to my son daily about what I'm reading, learning and how it matters in my life, and I ask him about what he's reading and learning, too.
I read at work or when my son is at school.	I don't talk to my son about my reading or ask him about his reading, but I do tell him he needs to read because it's important, and sometimes I barter with him to get him to read.
I sometimes flip through a magazine while waiting in line at the supermarket or sitting in a doctor's office.	I tell my son he doesn't have to read if he has other things to do.
No reading here; I haven't read since I graduated high school/college.	I talk negatively about reading within earshot of my son and even in front of him.

Did you feel it? The only congruent combination is "I read books/ other reading material in front of my son every day" and "I talk to my son daily about what I'm reading, learning and how it matters in my life, and I ask him about what he's reading and learning, too." It has the action and the words working in concert.

On the other hand, if you read in front of your son but barter with him, let him off the hook, or talk negatively about reading, even if you mumble to yourself, you'll lose credibility in his eyes. Boys also have trouble when they're told by someone else that reading is important, but they've never seen that person read.

As I shared earlier, your son pays attention to your words *and* actions to make his decision about reading. Inconsistency on your part gives him permission to keep protecting himself from the pain/boredom/dislike of reading. Boys don't just follow the path they're told to follow, and neither will your son; he must first make sure you're in the driver's seat, sitting beside him, with skin in the reading game. By watching to see if you walk your reading talk, your son gauges if he can trust you and how safe he is, and he'll only read if he feels safe that you "get it."

Because you walk the talk... your son will trust that you value reading books.

Once the boys I taught learned the vocabulary of emotions and found their voice, they shared with me the conflicted reading moments and messages they had received over the years. When they had been unable to express their hurt and confusion over what was being said or done, the easiest solution for them at the time was to sever all ties with reading. Most boys decided that, because their parents seemed to value other things more highly (for example, following directions, being good, reading "appropriate" material, sports, not being bothered over his reading), he didn't need to read.

Below I share snippets of what many boys shared with me over the years. It's a starting place to better understand your son's heart and how he may be interpreting your words and actions. After you read each statement, take a moment and imagine how *you* might have responded if this was something your son had said to you.

Boys' Snippets, highlighting *not* Walking the Talk

- I couldn't sit still during reading time, and I used to kind of stand and sit in my chair because it was more comfortable. My teacher would send me out of the room because it annoyed her, making me miss reading time because I just couldn't sit. When my mom came home from parent/teacher conferences, she grounded me for not sitting during reading time, like my teacher asked.
- Every time I read comic books/graphic novels (which was a lot), my mom would always tell me to get something "more appropriate" to read, but when I wasn't reading, she didn't bother me. So I stopped reading, and now she leaves me alone.
- At school, my teachers told me to read for homework, but nobody in my family reads books, so they didn't make me. As long as I left my homework assignment book on the kitchen table, my mom signed the spot that said I read for 30 minutes. This way, as she always said, we wouldn't get in trouble. Not that my teachers cared—they just checked to see if my mom signed and never asked questions about what I read. I never read a book in all my years at school. Not once.
- I used to read books real slow and needed to re-check them out of the school library each week. There was a girl in my

class, and she was the best reader and teacher's pet. She always made fun of me, calling me turtle and slowpoke, even in front of the teacher. She never got in trouble. When I stopped checking out books, she stopped making fun of me. My mom never asked me why I didn't take out books from the school library anymore.

- My dad never read a book in his whole life, and looks at me funny when he catches me reading. He told me I don't have to read books if I don't want to, because there are better things to do, like watch football. Now I watch the games with my dad and do other stuff.
- I hate books. When I try to read, the words jump off the page, I skip lines, and I can never tell where I should be on the page. I tried telling my mom and my teachers, but they said there was nothing wrong with my eyes. Once I decided to stop reading books, my eyes were fine.
- I once read a book on the school bus, and a group of older boys made fun of me and called me a girl. They took the book and messed it up a bit. My teacher gave me a detention because I didn't take good care of her book. When I told my mom, she said not to read on the bus anymore and the bullies would leave me alone. I don't want to be a girl, so I stopped reading.
- My mom used to read aloud to me before I went to sleep every night. Then when I was in second grade she stopped and said I should be reading books by myself. And that was it. I miss her reading to me. I thought reading and talking about books was our thing. Now I don't really care about books because she never asks me about them anymore.
- In third grade my reading score was basic. In fourth grade, my teacher put me in a special group to help me pass the test. We worked in workbooks and on the computer. But I didn't pass again. In fifth grade, I had to come to school early in the

morning to keep practicing. And I still didn't pass. My mom said it's okay because soccer is my thing, not reading. I just wasn't born a reader.

Reading and imagining these moments can help you begin to see how you may be unintentionally devaluing reading through your words and actions. Rehearsing new ways of responding to your son in these types of moments allows you to reshape and rewrite your message about the value of reading. Because when you reshape your *thinking* about reading, you will also reshape how you *talk* about reading to your son.

Because you walk the talk... you'll be able to reflectively listen and respond to what your son is saying about reading.

One way to tell if your son is picking up on unintended messages about the four types of reading is by really listening to how he responds when you suggest that he read for pleasure. Does he utter anything like the following statements about reading?

Reading is boring and stupid... I hate reading... There aren't any books that I like to read... I'd rather be _____ ... I already have too much homework where I have to read... Why do I have to read this dumb, girly book for my teacher... I read in school... We only need to read for standardized tests... Only nerds read books, and I'm cool.

If so, it's important to reflect on how you answer him when he says these things. Below are ways *I* used to respond to boys when they said these things to me. Maybe you'll find yourself saying the same or similar things.

- *Reading is boring and stupid...* No it's not, reading is fun. Just do it.
- *I hate reading...* We don't say the word hate here, so don't ever say you hate reading.
- *There aren't any books that I like to read...* How can you say there's nothing to read? Look at all the books in our classroom and school library you can choose from.
- *I'd rather be _____...* Well, you're not, so get reading.
- *I already have too much homework where I have to read...* Well, reading is my homework, too, so you just need to read some more.
- *Why do I have read this dumb, girly book for my teacher/ English class?* Books for girls aren't dumb. Keep reading.
- *I already read in school...* And you're going to read at home, too. End of story.
- *We only need to read for standardized tests...* Who told you that lie? When you grow up, you'll still need to read for work.
- *Only nerds read books, and I'm cool!...* People who read books are not nerds. I read, and I'm not a nerd.

As you might guess, my combative, dismissive talk didn't help boys to develop a positive attitude toward reading or help me to help them recognize the four different types of reading. If anything, I just added to the mess.

Nothing in my responses showed the boys that I believed in them or that they could trust my walk and feel safe with me in the driver's seat. At the time, I didn't realize that my words pushed them to shut down and move further away from reading for pleasure.

It turns out that I wasn't listening to what boys were expressing about their relationship with reading, and my talk shows it. Instead of helping them make sense of what they were saying, I inadvertently reinforced their negative comments as being acceptable and true for them.

It took closely reading and practicing the exercises in *How to Talk So Kids Will Listen & Listen So Kids Will Talk* (by Adele Faber and Elaine Mazlish) for me to deeply understand what was involved in listening and to become trustworthy and credible when boys talked about reading.

I no longer thoughtlessly jumped right in when they shared negative reactions towards reading. I learned how using simple words and phrases like "oh" or "mmm" or "I see" gave me time and space to respond more intentionally. I also discovered that when I listened, if I turned and faced the boys so that I could look respectfully into their eyes as I spoke, it mattered a lot to them.[32]

Here is an example of how my *listening* changed and therefore, so did my talk.

Reading is boring and stupid... "Mmm. For you, would you say it's more boring or more stupid? ... I see, you think it's boring *and* stupid. Would you mind sharing with me a bit more about when you think reading is the most boring and stupid for you? ... Oh, I want to make sure I have this right. So when you need to read for social studies, you get bored and can't focus. Then your stupid teacher makes you feel dumb because you don't know the answer. Are there other times reading is boring and stupid? ... Mmm. Just when you need to read for social studies. I see."

In this example, when I listened and mirrored back what I thought I had heard, I uncovered the tangled hot mess of confusing reading for pleasure with mandatory reading. It is only through paying attention and asking open-ended, prompting questions that I am in a position of being able to help him untangle the difference between reading for social studies and reading for pleasure. Without having skin in the reading game (being willing to dive deep and be temporarily uncomfortable), I would have missed this.

Because you walk the talk... your reading message will influence your son's attitude towards reading.

I'm going to explain this ripple effect through a very powerful story.

Early in my career, I had a student who was a cool kid to teach, except during "choice" reading time. He thought reading for pleasure was stupid and for stupid people. I know because he told me that over and over again.

After trying everything, I called in his parents for help.

The first question his dad asked me (with his arms crossed) was whether his son knew how to read words and comprehend them. I told him yes. He asked if I thought his son would do fine on the standardized test. I told him yes. Then he asked, "Why are we here?"

I explained that his son wouldn't read during "choice" reading time and that I was concerned as to why he was not reading for pleasure. The dad then made it clear that *he* never read a book just to read a book, and he was successful. He read what he needed to, and no one was going to tell his son he had to read books if he didn't want to. This dad's walk and talk to his son was, "To be successful in the world, reading skills are what you need, and reading for pleasure isn't necessary."

His son took this message to heart because his dad was credible and trustworthy in his eyes. His dad both walked and talked non-reading in every sense of the word, totally negating my message that "To be successful in this world, reading books for pleasure *does* matter."

When the dad realized how his influence had played out in the classroom (the real world) versus how it played out at home (privately), he made some significant shifts in his reading walk and talk. Once he started to read books at home in front of his son and talked positively about reading for pleasure, his son started to read for pleasure, too.

Parents matter. Consciously or unconsciously (and as a reader or a non-reader), they have the greatest influence on how their son views the cultivation of the reading habit in *his* life. Taken together, believing, investing and reading gather the momentum necessary so that a shift in your reading mindset becomes a real possibility. Paying attention to how you listen and talk to your son about reading keeps the momentum moving forward.

ACTION STEPS

1. Tough Question: Do you walk the talk in a credible, trustworthy way?

It's not enough to just talk reading or walk reading, you must synchronize the two so they work together in harmony. When you do that, your son will believe you mean what you say and you say what you mean. In his eyes, that equals credible and trustworthy, and only then does he feel safe to follow your lead.

2. Digging deep: How do others view your reading habit?

Throughout my career, it always surprised me when I discovered that how I viewed myself varied drastically from how others viewed me. Instead of running from those moments (even though I wanted to), I used the opportunity to dig deep, become aware, and grow as a person and educator for the boys in my charge. It's important that you do the same for your son.

Below I'm going to share a couple of different scenes with you, followed by asking you to think about yourself. This is my take on the Johari window tool typically used in business settings to help people better understand their relationship with themselves and others. I use it here to open you up to seeing your reading from your son's and others' perspectives.

Maybe you still see yourself as a frequent reader (someone who reads almost every day), and so does your mother, because at one point in your life you always had your nose in a book, but in reality, you haven't read a book since your son was born, a decade ago. *He* only knows you as an infrequent reader (someone who doesn't read books).

Or maybe you pretend to be a moderate reader (someone who reads a few times a month) because you're part of a book club, but you actually hate reading. So every time your son sees you read, he also hears you curse a bit and roll your eyes and talk about "stupid books." You don't realize he's listening and absorbing what you are saying.

Your book club, on the other hand, thinks you love to read and discuss books. Or maybe you're like the dad I introduced you to above—proud to be an infrequent reader, and your son's teacher sees how he is playing it out in public without your knowledge.

Do you see why it's important to become aware of and open to how others view your reading habit? You gain invaluable information of your "blind spots"—those things that are known by others, but you're unaware of them. In the first scene, the parent's mom would say she is a reader, but her son would say she isn't because she's not. In the second scene, the book club would say the parent is a reader, but the son knows the truth. And in the third scene, the teacher's perspective lets you in on how your son is publicly interpreting your talk.

- On a piece of paper or in the workbook, jot down how you think others might view your reading habit—your son, your son's teacher, your family, your boss, your colleagues, your best friend, your neighbors. Does everyone see your habit in the same way? Why or why not?
- (This is the part that requires grit, but it's very necessary to follow through on.) Ask a few different people from your list (your son being one of them) how they view you as a reader. Jot down what they say and compare it to what you thought they would say. Are there discrepancies? Digging deep at this point helps you understand the different ways you talk, or don't talk, about books, and when and where. When someone is a reader, they also talk positively about books to anyone, including their son. By asking others for their perspective, you'll discover to what degree that is true for you.
- The last step in the process is to become aware of your son's view compared to everyone else's, and take steps to bring more credibility to your talk. How does he see your reading life? Do you notice any mixed signals you may be sending him? Jot down two action steps you can include right away.

3. Rehearsal: Practice new responses to the following statements your son might say to you about reading.

Reading is boring and stupid... I hate reading... There aren't any books that I like to read... I'd rather be (playing football, watching TV, _____) ... I already have too much homework where I have to read... Why do I have to read this dumb, girly book for my teacher... I read in school... We only need to read for standardized tests... Only nerds read books, and I'm cool.

- Choose one reading statement that you resonate with the most.
- Imagine that you're suggesting to your son that he read a book and he responds with that statement.
- First, think about what your typical rebuttal to his statement would be. Play it out in your mind.
- Now *rewrite* the scene in your notebook or workbook. Your son stays the same, but this time *you* change. Instead of your typical rebuttal, you listen reflectively and respond intentionally. You now know boys listen better if you look at them respectfully, use small words like mmm to show you're listening, and ask follow-up questions to start untangling his hot mess. Knowing your son, imagine how he might respond to your questions and use his words to guide your next thought. Using my example as a guide, write your response.

Reading is boring and stupid... "Mmm. For you, would you say it's more boring or more stupid? ... I see, you think it's boring and stupid. Would you mind sharing with me a bit more about when you think reading is the most boring and stupid for you? ... Oh, I want to make sure I have this right. So when you need to read for social studies, you get bored and can't focus. Then your stupid teacher makes you feel dumb because you don't know the answer. Are there other times reading is boring and stupid? ... Mmm. Just when you need to read for social studies. I see."

- For extra practice, do the same with the other reading statements. The more you think through, the more flexible you'll become with your responses.
- Next, say the responses out loud. If you have another person to practice with, great. If not, practice on your own. It's important to not skip this step. The more you practice your responses out loud, the better you'll get at using them.
- When you feel ready to stretch, ask your son to read a book and see what he says. Try out your response with him. Gauge how you feel and pay attention to how he reacts. Write down any insights you learned from your conversation. Remember, this is not about transforming your son's non-reading habit into the reading habit, yet. This is for you to practice how you listen and talk to him about reading.

KEY TAKEAWAYS... Building Block 4: Walk the Talk

- You're only credible in your son's eyes when you *walk* reading by showing him its importance in *your* life and *talk* reading by discussing what you read in a positive way.
- The only way you can legitimately reshape how your son values reading is by becoming aware of how you may be unintentionally devaluing it yourself.
- The only viable ways to gain the information needed to re-define reading for your son is to learn how to listen reflectively and intentionally respond to his statements about reading.
- Be aware of the reading message you are sending out to your son; you greatly influence his perception of reading.

By walking the talk, you've set yourself up as a credible reading resource in your son's eyes. Now it's time to dig deep in Building

Block 5: Prioritize to understand what leisure activities you are currently valuing and spending the most time engaging in besides reading.

Visit the following link to download the "Tune-In to Chat" exercise that I created for you.

The "Tune-In to Chat" exercise explains different ways to approach your preteen/early teen son and talk to him about reading and books.

http://www.hillarytubin.com/freetuneinexercise

❧ BUILDING BLOCK 5: PRIORITIZE ❧

Your son needs you to give the same priority to reading
as you do for other things that you enjoy doing.

THE RIPPLE EFFECTS OF PRIORITIZING

**Because you prioritize... you'll show your son reading
matters in your life and in his life, too.**

To grasp why reading for pleasure should be a priority in your day, the **2014 US Labor Census: American Time Use Survey** results are food for thought and a great place to begin. For American adults who live with kids that are 6–17 years old, the following chart shows the average time in hours/minutes per day they spend in leisure and sports activities, and in helping with kid-related activities.[33]

Activity	Adult Average in Households with Kids
Watching TV	2 hours 30 min.
Socializing and communicating	48 min.
Other leisure sports activities, including travel	31 min.
Playing games and computer use for leisure	25 min.
Participating in sports, exercise and recreation	21 min.
Travel time for kid-related activities	15 min.
Relaxing/Thinking	15 min.
Physical care of kids	14 min.
Helping kids with homework	13 min.
Reading for leisure	**13 min.**
Talking to/with kids	**5 min.**
Reading to/with kids	**1 min.**

American Time Use Survey, released on Wednesday, June 24, 2015

The activity table is ordered from the most amount to the least amount of time spent each day in an activity. I have emphasized (bold type) the three critical daily activities that are needed to ensure that boys will read: reading to/with boys; talking to/with boys; and reading for leisure in front of boys. Only 19 minutes total per day are allocated to reading and talking to kids. And, without knowing whether the parents are reading when and where their son can see them, the 13 minutes a day of leisure reading may not be making the kind of difference it could be.

On the other hand, the table clearly shows that in many homes, watching television and socializing have a higher priority than reading for pleasure. When their parents relegate reading and talking to them to the bottom of the priority list, preteen and early teen boys know, see, and feel this. It can't be hidden, swept under the carpet or brushed over. It's reality, and they know it.

Think about the statistics shared in the Introduction: globally, US boys are 23rd in reading literacy and only about 25% of preteen and early teen boys self-report that they are frequent readers. Since we know that parents' reading frequency is one of the most powerful predictors of a boy's reading frequency, those statistics are not really surprising when one sees how people with kids are actually spending their time.

ACTION STEPS

1. Tough Question: Do you prioritize reading in the same way as you do for other leisure activities you enjoy (watching television, playing sports, relaxing, socializing, etc.)?

As you can tell from the survey, most Americans don't prioritize reading, so if that describes you, you're not alone. My hope is that, after reading the first part of this book, Developing the Boy-Responsive Reading Mindset, you will have a deeper understanding of why a shift in your daily schedule and priorities is imperative for your son's reading habit.

2. Estimate the amount of time you engage in each activity on the chart: This action step makes the invisible visible, so you can find a way to include reading in your day. It's not meant to be an exact science; it's just meant to give you a sense of your time and how it's currently being utilized. The goal here is to think about your son. However, if you have other children, I included a row to fill in time spent with them. If you engage in a leisure activity or sport that is not included, add it in the box labeled "other."

- In your notebook or the workbook, jot down your times.
- Starting with the first activity, reading to/with your son, how much time each day do you spend on this activity? Don't over-think this; it's only an estimate. Write the time.
- Do this for each activity.
- Lastly, re-organize your activity table, starting with the activity you engage in the most down to the one you engage in least.

(To grasp what this will look like, see the table on the next page.)

Activity	Your Time in hours/ mins	Average Person Time
Reading to/with your son		1 min
Talking to/with your son about books and complicated social issues		5 min*
Reading for pleasure in front of your son		13 min*
Helping your son with homework		13 min
Physical care of your son		14 min
Travel time for kid-related activities		15 min
Relaxing/Thinking		15 min
Participating in sports, exercise and recreation		21 min
Playing games and computer use for leisure (not social media)		25 min*
Other leisure sports activities including travel		31 min
Socializing and communicating (face-to-face, phone, texting, social media, email)		48 min*
Watching TV		2 hrs 30 min
Total time with children other than your son		N/A
Other:		N/A

*For the purpose of the following exercise, adaptations to the activity have been made.

3. Reflect on and re-allocate the time you spend on leisure and sports activities, and helping with kid-related activities: By filling in the above activity chart, you become open to seeing your daily schedule in a new way. This new way allows for reflection on how you prioritize your time and the opportunity to re-allocate how you use the time in your day. The reflecting and re-allocation process loosens up and shifts your mindset so that frequently reading for pleasure becomes a real and tangible possibility.

Reflecting on Time: The questions below will lead you to important insights about your current habits and what your son sees you prioritizing and valuing, perhaps unintentionally.

• Which activity do you engage in the most? How much time do you spend doing it? Do you enjoy it? Why/why not?
• Which activity do you engage in the least? How much time do you spend doing it? Do you enjoy it? Why/why not?
• Which activities do you currently prioritize and make happen every day, no matter what? In total, how much time do you spend on those activities? Write down some thoughts on why you prioritize each of these activities.
• Is there an activity you engage in, but don't particularly enjoy? If yes, which one? How much time do you spend doing it?
• Which activities do you spend more time doing than the average person does? Write down some thoughts on why you think that's so.
• Which activities do you spend less time doing than the average person does? Write down some thoughts on why you think that's so.

- Which activities does your son see you engaged in the most? The least?
- Are these the same/similar activities your son engages in during his leisure time? Which ones?
- Do your above answers line up with the priorities and values you wish to pass on to your son? Why/why not?

Playing with Time: The questions below are structured for re-allocating your schedule to include reading for pleasure when and where your son can see you.

- What time does your son leave for school? What time does he arrive home? Does he play sports/have committed activities on the weekends? If your son's schedule changes each day, make sure to note the different times.
- If you work outside the home, what time do you leave for work? What time do you arrive home? Any regular commitments and/or activities on the weekends?
- Write down the days of the week (Sunday, Monday, Tuesday, Wednesday, Thursday, Friday, Saturday). Next to each day, write down the times you and your son won't be together in the same space. Use your information from the above questions. Blocking out time constraints, commitments and demands means you won't put reading for pleasure in competition with other important activities in your life. Without planning ahead this way, reading may inadvertently get put to the side, rather than become the priority it needs to become.
- Write down the days of the week again. Next to each day, write down all the times you and your son will be together and available in the same space (house and car (e.g. book on tape)).
- Using the schedule above, look at each day individually, starting with Sunday. Visualize the day as it typically unfolds.

What are you doing? What is your son doing? Now imagine the same day and see yourself reading something you find enjoyable, somewhere you find comfortable, instead of doing something you normally do that is not a priority. Determine the time. Is it morning, afternoon, evening? Write down your answer under Sunday, and then move to Monday. Follow the same steps for the rest of the week.

- The most important step: schedule 10–15 minutes to read each day and write it on your calendar or put it on your phone with an alarm.

KEY TAKEAWAYS... Building Block 5: Prioritize

- Understanding what you prioritize in your day, in a visible, tangible way, opens up space for you to discover where you can include reading for pleasure.
- When you re-allocate your time to include reading in your day, your son will notice and become aware of your changing priorities. This action on your part will allow him to shift the way he uses his time and include reading in his day, too.

Congratulations! You have now developed a boy-responsive reading mindset.

This means that you:

1. Believe your son will read.
2. Are invested and have skin in the reading game.
3. Know it's important to become your son's reading role model and have started reading.
4. Understand that, to be a credible reading resource for your son, you must walk the reading talk.
5. Took the time to prioritize your schedule to include reading for pleasure in a visible way.

You're ready to venture forward and begin creating the boy-responsive reading environment your son needs starting with Building Block 6: Appreciate.

Visit the link below for the "Prioritize Your Schedule" template I created for you.

The "Prioritize Your Schedule" template will help you to organize your responses to the Action Step: Playing with Time.

http://www.hillarytubin.com/freescheduletemplate

❧ BUILDING BLOCK 6: APPRECIATE ❧

Your son needs you to appreciate what he reads
and how he reads.

THE RIPPLE EFFECTS OF APPRECIATING

Because you appreciate... your son will discover what makes reading fun, valuable and even worth doing for a lifetime.

Recently, I conducted an informal reading survey with men between the ages of 35–60. I asked them if they read in the last six months, and if so, what they read. Most men said they didn't read at all, some said they only read work documents and/or the newspaper, and a few were avid, frequent readers.

Below are the types of books the avid male readers read in the last six months:

✓ Comic Books/ Graphic Novels
✓ Post-Apocalyptic
✓ Dystopia
✓ Fantasy
✓ Horror
✓ Biography
✓ Business

The avid readers also had at least one parent who was a frequent reader. They considered themselves frequent readers when they were kids and had been basically reading the same types of fiction books back then, too. When asked how their parents reacted to their book choice, all said that they never felt judged or limited. Because their parents were open to and respectful of their choices, all agreed to being more open and willing to read mandatory and recommended books in high school and college. These males also attributed their current success at work and in life to having been avid readers since they were young, and they recognized that they're constantly relying on their strong reading and communication skills, vocabulary, and verbal cognitive ability to accomplish their professional and personal goals.

The rest of the males shared that they couldn't remember if their parents read; they never read as kids; and the only books they remembered reading were "forced" on them by their English teachers. Many "read" (mostly skimmed) their college readings, and now they read for work. Even with success in their chosen professions, they all wished they had read more as a kid and enjoyed reading now. All of them agreed they feel like they missed/are missing out on something. When I asked why they don't read now, many of them said they just can't find a book they like or the time to fit reading into their schedule.

Everything about my reading conversations with adult males was eerily similar to my conversations with 9- to-14-year-old boys. Not surprising. Because without a huge shakeup—without someone taking the wheel, investing, becoming a reading role model, walking and talking, and appreciating what they read—nothing will change, and these men are proof of that assertion.

It took Dr. Lawrence Sipe, my brilliant education and literature professor, to teach me how to shift my mindset about boys, what they love to read and their reading habit. He is the one who opened me up to truly appreciate and say a resounding yes—and really mean it—to boys reading picture books, comic books, graphic novels, humorous books, lots of plot and action (fantasy), only male protagonists, series, informational text, and reading the same book over and over and over again. Because of him, I also learned the extraordinary value of Captain Underpants and the other series books my boys devoured, such as Time Warp Trio, Goosebumps, Series of Unfortunate Events, Artemis Fowl, Percy Jackson and the Olympians, Diary of a Wimpy Kid, 39 Clues, and Harry Potter.

Since *my* favorite books were character-driven, literary fiction novels (usually historical) with a strong female protagonist, I must admit that it wasn't easy to let go of what I considered "appropriate" and not "privilege," my tastes, or the Literary Canon, just because I was the adult in the room. You might find yourself grappling with this or something similar, too—wanting your son to read, but also needing to interfere with and control what he prefers to read.

So what transformative, *Karate Kid*-type wisdom did Dr. Sipe share, forever changing my mindset?

He said that it's all about where I focus my attention. If I only focus on the book, all I'll see is the book. If I only focus on the boy, all I'll see is the boy. Instead, when my full attention centers on how engaged boys are with reading the material of their choice, nothing else will matter. How true!

Here's what my full attention noticed time and time again:

A boy reading a book **I deemed appropriate** looked like this:

eyes on the clock, flipping pages, sighing while reading, forgetting the book at home, and shrugging his shoulders when asked about it. Very painful, as I explained in Building Block 2: Invest.

A boy reading a book *he* **chose** looked like this: eyes on the book, cracking up while reading, missing recess and lunch to keep reading, getting to school early to tell me about something he read, reading it again, and showing his friends parts of the book and recommending it. 100% pleasure.

Observing the dramatic divide between mandatory/pain reading versus reading for pleasure hurt at first; then it wowed me. Hurt, because it was clear boys weren't interested in my recommended books (Ouch!), and wowed me because it was like a completely different boy was reading.

Dr. Sipe was right. By centering my full attention on a boy's degree of engagement with what he was reading while he transformed his non-reading habit into the reading habit, I saw just how painful the other types of reading (foundational, standardized and mandatory) are for a self-proclaimed non-reading boy. And even though I meant well with my recommendations during the early phases of their reading habit transformation, I was part of the problem, not the solution.

To get you started thinking about what your son may want to read, below are some results from the 2015 Scholastic Report:

- 93% of kids ages 9–14 say that their favorite books are the ones that they have picked out themselves; they're also most likely to finish reading a book that they have picked out themselves.
- 76% of boys ages 9–11 say they would read more if they could

find more books they like, and 79% of boys ages 12–14 say the same thing.

- Some reasons boys ages 9–14 have for choosing the books they want to read: it makes them laugh; it has a mystery or a problem to solve; it tells a true story (informational text); it's something they're interested in; it's a favorite book that they enjoy reading again and again; they want to challenge themselves; they saw the movie and want to read the book.

Boys' Favorite Series and Books

- Ages 9–11: Harry Potter, Diary of a Wimpy Kid, Captain Underpants, Goosebumps, Percy Jackson, Geronimo Stilton, Wayside School, Magic Tree House, and The Boxcar Children
- Ages 12–14: Harry Potter, Percy Jackson, Diary of a Wimpy Kid, Artemis Fowl, Eragon, The Chronicles of Narnia[34]

Here are some other favorite authors and series that my boys loved over the years: Gary Paulson, Jerry Spinelli, Carl Hiaasen, Louis Sachar, Roald Dahl, Jon Scieszka, James Patterson (yes, he even writes for kids), anything Greek Myth-related, and Maximum Ride, to name a few.

Through awareness, understanding and appreciation, your son will have the opportunity to grow into a lifetime reader. Think about the difference between the successful grown men in the informal reading survey. The non-readers felt reading was "forced" on them since they were kids, and today they feel like they're missing out on something. On the other hand, the readers read whatever they wanted to as kids, and today they feel accomplished because of their reading.

Boys are not so complicated; their reading needs are actually quite simple. When boys believe that their preferences are appreciated, they will become readers, and when their preferences are *not* appreciated, they will become self-proclaimed non-readers.

Because you appreciate... your son will recognize that reading material comes in a variety of forms.

Boys carry the misconception that "real" reading only happens when they read fiction paperback and hardcover books. Anything else is not worthy or considered reading. This belief is very limiting for them when it comes to developing their reading habit, and it's important to help your son understand what else is available for him to read.

Below are other forms/media your son can and should read:

- Newspapers (hardcopy)
- Magazines (hardcopy)
- Books, newspapers, magazines on E-readers (Kindles and Nooks or iPads that are distraction free, i.e. they have no access to the internet, apps, games or music)
- Audiobooks (yes, listening to books on tape is a viable choice)
- Printed from the computer (articles and blogs found prior to reading time, printed onto paper to read during reading time)
- Short stories or anthologies around a topic
- Comic books or graphic novels

If your son struggles with reading, he still must be reading for pleasure every day, too. Research finds that this is a critical piece that must be in place for struggling readers, or they will keep struggling.[35] Audiobooks work great, and Kindle also has a text-to-speech option available for many of their books. If your son can listen and read at the same time, that's the best option (visit the link at the end of this chapter for more information about preteen and early teens reading on an e-reader).

Reading aloud to your son is another great option, even if he's 14 years old. This is not the time for him to read out loud to you or for you to ask him questions; it's meant to be a comfortable, safe and pleasurable time for your son. Many times, I only needed to read the first few pages or first chapter aloud to get boys started. Some parents found that when they read mandatory reading material aloud to their son, he actually engaged more, did better with the subject, and eventually was able to read it on his own.

Another option I used is a bit antiquated, but it worked magic, especially if you don't always have time to read aloud to your son when the two of you are together: read what they chose into a tape recorder or the voice memo on your cell phone. Many of my struggling readers became independent readers this way. One boy badly wanted to read the sports page of the local newspaper, but he couldn't. Every morning I bought the paper before school, read 30 minutes of articles into the tape recorder for him, and then he was able to listen and read at the same time. I only needed to do this for 3 weeks before he broke the code of the sports page and could read it on his own (to learn more, visit this link: www.hillarytubin.com/freemystory.pdf).

It's important for you to become comfortable with and know the different forms of material your son can read. When you do, you'll be able to give him permission and support to expand his definition of "real" reading.

Because you appreciate... research finds your son's reading achievement will significantly improve.

Recently, I asked a boy in seventh grade (a football player and video game fanatic) how many books he had read in the last 6 months. He responded, "Two books for summer reading, and maybe three if comic books count." When I asked him how many books he had read since third grade, he said, "Maybe 10 books total"; he couldn't really remember. His school has a library. He's walking distance from the public library and Barnes and Noble. His mom, dad and sisters read, just not always in front of him. So what is stopping him from reading?

I asked him, "What would get you reading for 15–30 minutes every day, between going to football practice and playing your video games?"

He said, "If I could read something I like and sit where I want."

But is it really that simple? His mom didn't think so, when I told her. She felt that because reading isn't held in high regard by his friends or community, he won't read even though both she and her husband both believe the reading habit is important.

This mom isn't alone in her thinking. I've heard many moms share this as the reason their sons don't read, but my experience shows otherwise. Boys will read, given choice in what they read and where they read in their home, no matter what their friends and community thinks. Peer effect does matter, but what happens in their home matters too.

Boys' underperformance in reading is now a global concern. The OECD (Organization for Economic Co-operation and Development, to which the United States belongs) recently wrote a report called, "Tackling Underperformance Among Boys." The report highlights specifically why boys are globally underachieving in reading, and what can be done to change this trajectory. Of course the most obvious reason boys are underperforming is because they are not reading for pleasure every day; PISA supports the finding that boys need to read for pleasure for around *30 minutes a day to significantly improve their reading achievement.*[36]

According to PISA statistics, reading fiction several times a week is the great equalizer for the boys: those who did read fiction scored 36 points (equivalent to one grade level) higher than boys who didn't. Statistics also found that, if US boys liked to read as much as US girls, their predicted reading performance average would be 24 points higher.[37]

We also know that, besides reading, boys are playing video games and engaging in other activities on a daily basis, but these activities don't provide the same benefits as reading does or raise their reading performance scores. One very surprising finding the OECD discovered: the kind of video game and the frequency with which it is played is what determines its impact on academic performance. It turns out that a student who plays one-player video games in moderation performs better than students who play these types of games every day or not at all. However, those students who play collaborative online games, no matter the frequency—a little, sometimes, or a lot—perform worse than students who never play collaborative games at all.[38]

I bring this up here, because there is definitely a prevalent misconception about video games. Many parents shared with me their positive take on their sons playing the collaborative video games instead of playing one-person video games: "At least they're being social and interacting with friends." Unfortunately, research finds that the negative effect of not reading is actually being exacerbated by playing collaborative video games, not the reverse.

"I'd read if I could read something I like and sit where I want."—Seventh grade boy reader

The OECD report also agrees with the boy above when it comes to allowing boys to read what they like. Yes, the type of text and the complexity of it makes a difference—those who frequently read fiction books as their primary reading material, plus a variety of other materials (magazines, newspapers, non-fiction texts, and comic books/graphic novels) perform the best (about 60 points higher)[39]—but here's what's really surprising and important to fully grasp:

1) Boys who frequently read comic books/graphic novels as their primary reading material and a variety of other reading materials (magazines, newspapers, and non-fiction texts), but no fiction, performed lower than the fiction readers, but **not too far behind them**.
2) Those who read other materials only (magazines, non-fiction texts and the newspaper), but did not read fiction or comic books/graphic novels, did better than those who didn't read at all, but not nearly as well as those who read those materials *with* fiction and/or comic books/graphic novels.[40]

To summarize:

- Reading fiction offers the best results, but comic books, graphic novels, magazines, non-fiction texts and/or the newspaper for 30 minutes a day also creates a huge return on investment (your son gains all the benefits reading offers) AND a substantial increase in his academic performance, when compared to not reading at all.

- One-player video games can and should be played in moderation—not in place of reading, but in conjunction with it to achieve the best results; collaborative video games hinder academic performance and need to be re-evaluated as a beneficial option for preteen and early teen boys.

As Dr. Sipe shared, it's not about what boys are reading, it's about their degree of engagement. Appreciating your son's reading preferences puts him on the path to success. Comic books/graphic novels, magazines, newspapers and non-fiction texts help him grow into the best version of himself, not the opposite.

Adding to the OECD Findings

My intensive research on early teen boys, books and the reading habit also confirms the OECD's findings.

During my 10 years of teaching middle school literacy, boys consistently started sixth grade with foundational reading (skills/comprehension), standardized reading and mandatory reading firmly in place. They all knew how to read words, answer teacher/workbook/multiple-choice questions about a text, and pretend to read a book just enough to get by.

All scored advanced or proficient on the state standardized reading test, and entered my classroom very proud of this fact. Yet, when I asked them to read books of their choice every night, many lost their minds and floundered miserably. Reading for pleasure was worse than torture, and caused great tension between us. Baffled, I dug deep into the data of their test scores, hoping to discover how this paradox was even possible.

Standardized reading tests have two types of questions: multiple-choice and open-ended. Multiple-choice questions typically have four answers to choose from, and most state standardized tests rely heavily on this type of question. Schools spend most of their reading time preparing boys for this part of the test by engaging them in heavy doses of foundational, standardized and mandatory reading, excluding reading for pleasure.

Open-ended questions are different from multiple-choice because there are no scaffolds (already provided answers) for support. This type of question requires a boy to bring all of his reading skills and what I call "mental sweat" to the table. To successfully respond, he needs to read and comprehend the entire grade-level passage and then use his higher-order thinking skills to figure out the answer (I break down what this means in Building Block 7: Balance).

I went back and studied the standardized tests of all the boys I had taught over the years to find out if a gap existed between their multiple-choice score (foundational, standardized and mandatory reading proficiency) and their open-ended score (pleasure reading proficiency). First, I separated the boys into two lists: self-proclaimed nonreaders and readers. Because boys, parents, teachers, administrators, government officials, and the newspapers only look at the overall score, I analyzed its components so that I could see more about their true proficiencies. I wrote down both their multiple-choice and open-ended scores from third, fourth, and fifth grade next to their name.

As I had hypothesized, the entire group of self-proclaimed *non-readers* had a huge gap between their multiple choice and open-ended scores. The average multiple-choice score was 90%, and the average open-ended score was 40%.

On the other hand, the boys who read for pleasure every day scored 90% or higher for *both* types of questions.

Over a three-year period (sixth, seventh and eighth grade), reading for pleasure was no longer optional. The boys chose what they wanted to read (content and form), but what wasn't a choice was reading for 30 minutes every night at home. Knowing the power of social interaction for boys, I also scheduled time every day for them to engage with their pleasure reading in a deeper, more profound way by chatting with their peers and with me.

By the end of sixth grade, open-ended scores doubled, and by eighth grade, those who read every night scored 90% or higher on those questions, closing the gap. The few boys who held tight to their self-proclaimed non-reading status still had high multiple-choice scores, but instead of improving, their open-ended scores stayed the same as they had been in elementary school or even decreased, which, to me, showed that reading for pleasure every night made a huge difference.

Because you appreciate… your son will feel appreciated as a reader and learn to appreciate others as readers.

To show you what I mean, I hope you don't mind if I tell you the story of two brothers I taught when they each were 9 years old.

Brother 1 loved fantasy. *A Wrinkle in Time* was a favorite. He read every fantasy book I owned, then moved on to historical fiction. His parents, avid readers themselves, purchased tons of fantasy and historical fiction books for Brother 1. By the time Brother 2 turned 9 years old, hundreds of books sat waiting for him to read, except Brother 2 wouldn't read them. Instead he declared that he hated reading, and whenever his parents told him it was time to read, he crossed his arms, pouted and said, "Make me!"

They became very concerned and asked me if I would talk to Brother 2.

When I started the conversation by asking, "How's it going?" his response went something like this: "I hate fantasy books. And I really hate historical fiction. Everything Brother 1 reads is so serious. Why does everyone want me to be like him and read his stupid, boring books?"

I knew this wasn't true, so I kept probing until he finally responded, "Everyone always talks about how smart Brother 1 is because of all the smart books he reads. No one ever says I'm smart or the books I want to read are smart." I remember this being music to my ears; Brother 2 wanted to read books, just not *his brother's* books.

So I asked, "What do you want to read?"

I can still see his huge smile and sparkling eyes when he answered, "Anything funny!"

Once Brother 2 learned that Captain Underpants, *Wayside School is Falling Down*, and joke books were valued and appreciated by his parents, just like Brother 1's books, everything changed.

He went from being a self-proclaimed nonreader to being an avid reader. By the end of the school year, Brother 2 even read many of Brother 1's favorite books from when he had been 9 years old. His parents told me that the two of them started talking every morning at breakfast about what they were reading. Brother 1 even lightened up a bit and read some of Brother 2's favorite humor books, and the family started learning and telling jokes at the dinner table. In high school, they both took honors English classes and went to great colleges, even though one started his reading habit with *A Wrinkle in Time* and the other with Captain Underpants.

Appreciate your son's reading choices today, fully and completely—without expecting him to be someone he's not—and he'll learn how to appreciate others as readers, as well.

Because you appreciate... your son will feel pleasure when he reads, not pain.

Choice matters for boys. Not just what they read, but also how and where they read. Below are ways boys prefer to read when they're reading for pleasure:

- Lying on the floor (on stomach or back)
- Sprawling in a beanbag chair or on pillows
- Leaning against a wall
- Outside
- Under something (a desk, a table, a chair, a pillow, a coat, a blanket)
- In a small space
- With a pet
- Using a flashlight
- In their bed

What's missing on this list? Sitting at a desk or table in a chair. For boys, this position equals pain, not pleasure, and is a reminder of foundational, standardized and mandatory reading in school. For pleasure reading to take hold in your home, it's important your son doesn't sit at a desk, unless he chose that spot. Encouraging him to find a reading spot where he feels comfortable for 30 minutes is key to overcoming any pain associated with how he's been made to read.

I do need to warn you that it can be tricky to appreciate how your son prefers to read. My appreciation definitely took some time. Even though I knew boys hated sitting at a desk to read, I felt more in control of their reading that way. Could I really trust preteen/early teen self-proclaimed non-reading boys to read squeezed behind the door or under their chair or leaning against a wall?

One favorite position boys used for reading (which I tried and hated) was lying on their back, with their arms stretched over their head and the book in both hands. I didn't believe they were reading, because for me it was so uncomfortable that I couldn't focus one bit. But they proved me wrong and were deeply engaged. The crazier I thought their location or position to be, the more engaged with reading they became.

Their pleasure was definitely my pain and vice-versa. And, as Dr. Sipe had taught me, boys being engaged with books is what I was going for, not my own comfort level.

Over the years, I heard about the greatest reading spots boys found with the help of their parents. One dad and his son built a treehouse together in their backyard as the reading spot. This was life-changing for the son, because before the treehouse he would not read, and after the treehouse, he read every day. The idea of the treehouse, reading about building and designing it together, and when it was complete, adding a cool lounge chair to read on (far away from his sister) became his new association with reading—one of pleasure.

Not everyone can (or wants to) build a treehouse in their backyard, but it's fun to start thinking outside the box for possible reading spots for your son—and for yourself, while you're at it.

ACTION STEPS

1. Tough Question: Do you appreciate *what* your son reads (comic books, magazines, manuals of something he enjoys, etc.) and *how* he reads (standing up, sprawled out on the floor or his bed, in a fort he makes, etc.)?

Appreciating takes being boy-responsive to a new level. This is the moment when any lingering notions you may have about reading for pleasure have to fly out the window. It's time to open up to a new world of reading. A world where your son says yes to the reading habit. A world where you can appreciate him reading comic books in a fort, or a skate board magazine in a treehouse, and not feel like you're a bad parent who's hurting your son's future success.

Now you know that, by appreciating his choices and meeting him where he is, you're giving your son the gift of a competitive edge and the foundation for a solid tomorrow.

2. Take Time to Explore Books Your Son Might Want to Read:

It's tough to practice appreciating what your son reads if he isn't reading. Or maybe you realize that every time he tried to read, you didn't show appreciation in his book taste. Let's change that, starting now.

Below is a simple, yet very powerful, process (OLBE) so you can begin to appreciate what your son might want to read before he even starts reading (you'll also end up with a great list of recommendations to share with him later):

- **Observe:** take time (I took a week) to pay attention to what types of activities/interests/hobbies your son enjoys today by watching what he does and listening to what he says (visit the link www.hillarytubin.com/freetuneinexercise for more information on how to do that).

- **List:** In a notebook or in the workbook, list the activities/ interests/hobbies your son enjoyed throughout the week. Here's an example of a possible list: football (playing and watching), cooking breakfast with his dad, building with Legos, picking on his sister, playing practical jokes, staring at the moon and stars, watching *The Simpsons*, playing Mine-Craft, Skyping with his grandpa, and reading comic books.

- **Brainstorm:** using what you learned in this chapter, coupled with the list of things your son enjoys, brainstorm a list of books/reading material in a variety of forms that you think your son might appreciate reading. Using the list above, here's an example: football strategy books, biographies of players, history of football, recipe books, Lego information printed from a computer, book on getting along with girls, joke books, funny books, astronomy books, stories about space, books on *The Simpsons* and other Simpson-related reading material, MineCraft books and instructions, and talk to his grandpa about possible book topics.

- **Explore:** there are many ways to explore your brainstorm list and find some book titles and options to jot down. For example, visit Amazon online, the public or school library, or talk to your son's teacher.

A great series to check out is Jon Scieszka's *Guys Read* anthology series. What's powerful and engaging about this series is how each volume covers a different theme (Sports Pages, Funny Business, Thriller, Other Worlds, True Stories, Terrifying Tales), with short stories written by top-notch authors. Not only will your son have a lot of variety to read, he'll also discover authors he might want to read more in-depth. I suggest visiting the website with the same name, GuysRead.com. This website is filled with great book titles, resources and fantastic ideas to help get your son reading.

Another helpful website is BoysRead.org.

3. Discover Out-of-the-Box Reading Spots:

Not only is it important to practice appreciating your son's book choices before he starts reading, it's also critical to practice appreciating how he reads best. OLBE will help you to think and plan ahead here too.

- **Observe:** every preteen/early teen boy has what I call a "comfort zone." This is the spot where he watched TV or played a video game for an extended period of time and/or a favorite spot where he likes to chill and veg out. Spend a few days observing where your son is at his most comfortable. Pay attention to his position and how long he stays in the spot. You'll gain a much better understanding of your son's natural inclinations and how he feels most comfortable.

- **List:** In a notebook or the workbook, keep track of the places he sits, his position and the duration.

- **Brainstorm:** walk around your house and imagine possible reading spaces by visualizing your son chilling and reading for pleasure in them. Don't forget to go outside, too. Using what you know about the way boys prefer to read, your son's "comfort zones," and the potential reading spaces you identified, jot down a list of possible reading spots.

- **Explore:** preteen/early teen boys love novelty, and reading spots can provide the necessary change. By thinking ahead and exploring cool options, you'll be prepared to shake things up by going on "reading field trips." Coffee shops and bookstores are classic ideas, but there are so many other great places to take boys to read. For example, if he loves comic books, take him to browse and read at a comic book store. Or if he loves the outdoors, how about a hike and time to read on a boulder by the water. Or head out on a bike ride, picnic and reading time. If you have a college campus nearby, take him there to read. Ask other people about possible "reading field trip" ideas. Jot down your ideas and keep adding to your list.

KEY TAKEAWAYS... Building Block 5: Appreciation

- When you appreciate the types of books boys like to read (comic books, humorous, series, true stories ...), your son will discover why reading is pleasurable.
- Many people believe reading only counts if they read a paperback or hard cover book. By appreciating the variety of forms "real" reading comes in (magazines, audiobooks, Kindles...), your son will begin to realize that what he reads counts, too.
- The best way for your son to improve his academic performance is by reading texts of his choice every day. In time, his reading appetite will grow to include more complex texts, but today, he just needs to read and enjoy it.
- If you want your son to appreciate other readers, he needs to know what it feels like to have his reading tastes appreciated.
- Boys don't like sitting at a desk to read. They prefer to lie down on the floor or lean or use a flashlight. Appreciating how your son feels comfortable reading means he'll associate reading with pleasure rather than pain.

Once you start to appreciate all that's available and interesting for your son to read, next up is getting real about his reading distractors in Building Block 7: Balance.

Visit the following link to download the "Kindle Cheat Sheet" I created for you.

The cheat sheet includes the positive benefits of your son reading on an e-reader, plus my recommendations of amazing unknown self-published Middle Grade and Young Adult authors found only on Amazon's Kindle Store.

http://www.hillarytubin.com/freeKindlecheatsheet

❧ BUILDING BLOCK 7: BALANCE ❧

Your son needs you to help balance his reading distractors.

THE RIPPLE EFFECTS OF BALANCING

Because you balance... you will recognize the 6 common reading distractors and how they influence your son's developing adolescent brain.

By prioritizing 10–15 minutes of reading for pleasure into your schedule, you model that behavior for your son long before you show him how to balance his own schedule. This opens him up to the idea, instead of immediately resisting it. He may still be angry, upset and sullen at what you're proposing (boys aren't fans of disruption in their schedules), but he won't stay that way very long; it will only *feel* like it's very long. The changes he noticed with his own eyes over the last 30 days are what will make the discussion about his reading habit possible.

Prior to discussing anything with your son, it's most important you first know and understand what reading distractors you're up against and their impact on your son if they are not in balance. I break them down into the *visible* distractors and the *invisible* distractors. Below are the most common reading distractors that preteen and early teen boys shared with me over the years, and they're a great place to start.

Visible Distractors

- **Competing Demands:** activities, hobbies, and commitments he either enjoys doing or is expected to do, such as sports (practice/game/with friends/alone) playing/practicing an instrument, after school activities (play rehearsal, chess, art, building, tutoring, religious classes, etc.), hanging out with friends. For some boys, girls are also a competing demand.
- **Homework:** depending on amount, grade, teacher, content area and/or his own abilities and motivation, this can take anywhere from 10 minutes to all night (studying for test, big projects, mandatory reading for multiple classes at the same time, procrastinating, etc.).
- **Technology/Media:** this includes watching TV/DVDs/videos, playing video games/apps, browsing on the computer for fun, visiting social networking sites, using a cell phone to talk or text, listening to music.

Invisible Distractors

- **Standardized Testing:** hidden pressure, too much, doesn't want to "fail," only sees reading as standardized reading (test prep, multiple choice questions, taking reading tests), views himself as a reader only based on his standardized test scores (advanced, proficient, basic or below basic)
- **Stereotyping:** doesn't identify with readers; he sees them as nerds/geeks who wear glasses, girls, the smart kids hanging out in the library, awkward and not athletic
- **Multitasking:** belief he can focus on and fully understand what is being read while doing any and all of the above distractors at the same time (for example: simultaneously read for pleasure, watch TV, listen to music and text a friend)

Early in my career, I knew that these six distractors interfered with my boys' reading for pleasure, but it was more annoying than worrisome. What I didn't grasp at the time were the distinct, life-long benefits that are only obtained through the act of reading for pleasure every day, starting in childhood. By not balancing the common distractors on one side of the scale with the 30-minute-a-day reading habit on the other, boys become vulnerable to what I call *underperformance disease*. Reading for pleasure is their only antidote, and they *need* you to make them take their medicine.

"We're suggesting that [kids are] missing something if they don't read but, actually, we're condemning kids to a lesser life. If you had a sick patient, you would not try to entice them to take their medicine. You would tell them, 'Take this or you're going to die.' We need to tell kids flat out: reading is not optional."—**Walter Dean Myers (Author)**

Research on the adolescent brain and how reading affects it offers a possible explanation. Below I highlight a few critical concepts that are relevant to the need for balance.

At age 12, your son's brain begins to literally transform. People think it's only hormones/puberty causing all the changes, but the adolescent's developing brain plays an important role, too.

In his book, *Brainstorm, The Power and Purpose of the Teenage Brain*, Dr. Daniel J. Siegel shares that "Adolescent change stems from how the brain is actually remodeling itself, pruning some connections, and laying down new pathways that increase the communication among remaining connections. This remodeling is shaped by how we focus our attention and live our lives."[41]

In her article, "Adolescent Brains are Works in Progress," Sarah Spinks states that adolescence is when the brain has great capacity to learn and excel in a variety of areas; however, adolescence is also the time that determines which specific neurons are going to survive or die. Depending on the type of activity the teenage brain is asked to do, the neural connections (synapses) will either be "exercised" and strengthened, or they will be pruned (just like tree branches) and weaken.[42]

In an interview in Frontline's *Inside the Teenage Brain* series, Dr. Jay Giedd (neuroscientist and adolescent brain expert) called pruning the "use it or lose it principle." When teens participate in activities like reading, music, sports, art or academics, those are the cells and connections that will be hardwired and survive. If they're lying on the couch or playing video games or watching TV, those are the cells and connections that are going to survive. **What teens do or don't do can actually affect the rest of their lives!**[43]

In the article "Short-and Long-Term Effects of a Novel on Connectivity in the Brain," researchers explain why including fiction reading in our lives matters. First, it strengthens and initiates neural activity and connectivity between two very important parts of the brain: the language-processing regions and the region responsible for higher mental and emotional processes, including memory, learning, speech and the interpretation of sensations. They also found people who read novels have what is known as a *lived-through experience* that stays with them beyond the time they are reading, and this may lead to being more empathetic in real life.[44]

People used to believe that by age six, the brain was pretty much set because it had almost reached adult size, and that the most important years were the first three. Now neuroscientists realize that a lot of important, dynamic developmental work is still happening in the brain between the ages of 3 and 16, and during the teenage years there's a great capacity for change. Dr. Geibb explains there are two times during which the brain overproduces cells and connections—in the womb and during pre-adolescence (ages 9, 10 and 11), which gives the brain a second opportunity and an enormous potential to learn, grow, and stretch.[45]

This matters tremendously because, around the age of 12, the brain's growing phase (with its amazing capacity to learn new things) winds down and the fierce competition begins to determine which of the weakest connections will be pruned. If he doesn't include reading for pleasure as part of his life now, your son is at risk of losing the critical neural connections that only this activity can produce in his brain. However, because you believe, invest, read, walk the talk, appreciate, and prioritize, your son's pleasure-reading connections have an excellent chance of survival.[46]

However, there's much more to consider. Your son's brain is not just growing and pruning connections right now. The frontal part of his brain—the home of judgment, organization, planning and strategizing—is also under construction. When left to make his own decisions, your son relies on his amygdala—the emotional, reactive and gut response center of his brain. Because of how his brain currently operates, your son desperately needs the benefit of your frontal lobe to help him balance it all and figure out with him what's important for his future success. Biologically, he's doing the best he can, but with your support, guidance, and modeling, he'll have the chance to learn by your example, while he exercises and strengthens the thinking and planning part of his brain, as well.[47]

"Learning by example is very powerful and that parents are teaching even when they don't realize they are teaching just by how they handle everyday aspects of their life... This is how most of the teaching is done. It's not when you set [sic] down at these special moments and have a conversation—it's the everyday moments that really have a huge impact on how the brain forms and adapts."—Dr. Jay Geibb, NIH researcher and neuroscientist

Because you balance... space will open up in your son's life to include 30 minutes of reading for pleasure every day.

Step one is recognizing and understanding the six common distractors. The next piece you need to understand up front is why 30 minutes of reading for pleasure every day is the sweet spot for your son. Knowing this will help you to make sure the scales are always balanced in your son's life and his pleasure reading is a constant. If not, you might cut corners some days because you're tired, or let pleasure reading slide because his distractor is being especially distracting.

In the OECD report they found that the biggest difference in reading scores were between the students who didn't read for enjoyment at all and those who read for 30 minutes a day.[48]

This finding is confirmed by a 1988 research study (plus subsequent studies), which shows that the amount of pleasure reading that occurs outside of school is the **best predictor of reading achievement**. The following chart analyzes what this means in numbers.[49]

Reading Frequency Chart		
Amount of Time Reading Per Day in Minutes	**Reading Achievement**	**Words Read Per Year**
21.1 minutes	90th percentile	1,823,000
14.2 minutes	80th percentile	1,146,000
9.6 minutes	**70th percentile**	**622,000**
6 seconds	**10th percentile**	**8,000**

Adapted from Anderson, Wilson, and Fielding (1988).

The more boys read, the more words they come across, and this is how cognitive stamina (the ability to sustain prolonged mental effort) is built, just like one builds a muscle by exercising it. Engaged, broad and deep reading requires stamina, endurance and agility, and that only happens with sustained practice every day.

This is why my sixth-grade boys were not able to cope with the open-ended questions on the state standardized reading test. All they had were themselves to rely on, and they couldn't do it without having the necessary scaffolds and support. Their years in school had taught them grade-level reading skills and trained them in the foundational, standardized and mandatory reading that the system supported. These are all important, but without 30 minutes of pleasure reading also happening every day, they did not have the opportunity to practice what they had learned in school while they were away from school, and they couldn't build cognitive stamina, endurance and agility.

Because you balance... your son will understand the cost/benefits of including 30 minutes of reading for pleasure in his day.

Now's a great time to remind you of the amazing benefits pleasure reading brings for your son and his brain and Tony Wagner's Seven Survival Skills:

Reading for Pleasure Benefits

- Strong verbal cognitive (thinking) and reading skills
- A more fully developed vocabulary, essential for increased communication skills
- An expanded background/general knowledge
- Improved writing/spelling/language/math skills
- Higher all-around academic achievement and test scores
- More fully developed empathy, essential for improving people skills
- A more fully developed imagination and intellectual curiosity
- Reduced stress

Tony Wagner's Seven Survival Skills

1. Critical thinking and problem-solving
2. Collaboration across networks and leading by influence
3. Agility and adaptability
4. Initiative and entrepreneurialism
5. Effective oral and written communication
6. Accessing and analyzing information
7. Curiosity and imagination

Screen Time Consumption: Boys' biggest distractor

In Building Block 2: Invest, I shared research from an article by Tom Corley called "16 Rich Habits." Mr. Corley found that one of the biggest differences between financially successful and financially struggling adults is their reading to screen time ratio.

The majority of wealthy adults read for 30 minutes a day and limited their screen time. On the other hand, almost all of the financially struggling adults did no reading during their day and watched at least an hour or more of TV, plus an hour or more of internet browsing.[50]

These findings are very similar to the results from the 2015 Scholastic Survey. Both parents and kids were asked the same question: How is time spent outside of school? Like the financially successful adults, 9- to 14-year-old frequent readers read books every day and balanced their screen time. This balance ultimately had them reading 10 times more books in a year than an infrequent reader did. That's because infrequent readers responded that (instead of reading) they spend their free time on an electronic device, game system, cell phone, watching TV, DVDs, and videos. Many also shared that they already read so much for school, they just don't feel like reading for fun.[51]

The 2015 *Common Sense Census: Media Use by Tweens + Teen* national survey conducted by Common Sense Media confirms how much technology and media are consuming the lives of 8- to 18-year-olds. Excluding media used for school or homework, they found 8- to 12-year-olds spent an average of 6 hours a day on using some form of media, with TV and XBox dominating for boys. Teens spent an average of 9 hours a day using some form of media, with listening to music, TV and Xbox dominating for boys. In addition, almost all teens said they multitask and think it has no effect on the quality of their work.[52]

As a teacher who has seen the low quality of multitasked work, I smelled it a mile away. I actually came to call this kind of work "dog poop," because it stank so bad. It wasn't until boys started seeing the difference in their own work when they stopped multitasking that they realized the fallacy of their prior thinking. Their reality check showed them the truth about their beliefs.

In the Introduction, I shared that a large percentage of preteen and early teen boys are self-reporting that they don't read for pleasure every day. The three national surveys the results came from show that the scales for the majority of preteen and early teen boys are heavily weighed down by TV, video games, and music. If you then add the other common distractors—homework (mandatory reading), standardized testing (standardized reading) and stereo-typing—a huge dilemma emerges, for two reasons.

Reason 1: As I stated above, when teens participate in activities like reading, music, sports, art or academics, those are the cells and connections that will survive and become hardwired. If they're lying on the couch or playing video games or watching TV, those are the cells and connections that are going to survive into adulthood.

Reason 2: Bobby Robson, an English soccer player and manager said, "Practice doesn't make perfect, practice makes permanent."

Acting as your son's temporary frontal lobe, this is when you need to ask yourself the following questions: What neural connections is he strengthening and exercising every day? What skills is he practicing every day and making permanent? Will these connections contribute to a successful future? Will these skills prepare him to survive and thrive in a global knowledge-based economy? Most importantly, do the benefits of reading for 30 minutes every day outweigh the cost of your son "giving up" something he might enjoy like playing video games, listening to music or watching television?

Your answers to these questions will help you help your son

understand the cost/benefits of including reading in his day.

Because you balance... your son will grow and accumulate an extensive vocabulary for his future success.

An extensive vocabulary is the foundation of strong literacy and communication skills, and strong literacy and communication skills are the foundation of success, especially in a knowledge-based economy.

If you asked a boy how someone learns vocabulary words for the long term, he most likely would say "by studying flashcards" or "by looking over words before a quiz." Unfortunately, his answer would be incorrect. These are both short-term methods (even though flashcards are the better option of the two), and are ineffectual for any lasting understanding and use. Check on him a week later and he'll only be able to retrieve some of the words. Check on him a month later and he'll remember nothing.

Studies have shown that exposure to a single word needs to occur multiple times before it is committed to long-term memory. That exposure includes seeing a word in context (printed text) multiple times, hearing it, becoming aware of it, learning the definition, and using it to speak and write.[53]

That's why the new SAT changed how vocabulary is now being tested. Instead of seeing words in limited contexts, complex vocabulary is now embedded in reading passages. To show college readiness, it is no longer enough to just know the definition of a word. Now your son will need to "reveal an understanding of relevant words in context and how word choice helps shape meaning and tone."[54]

Flashcards won't help anymore, but do you know what will make all the difference for your son? Not sports/art/musical instruments. Not technology. Not homework. Not standardized testing.

The only way for your son to grow and expand his vocabulary for the long term is by including 30 minutes of pleasure reading in his day.

Researchers, Drs. Cunningham and Stanovich, concluded that the number of pages you read contributes significantly to vocabulary knowledge. They found that the best way to grow an extensive vocabulary is by being exposed to "rare words"—words beyond the level of a fourth–sixth grader—and the best place to be exposed to them is in books or printed texts. This is because the more pages you read, the more rare words you come across per every thousand words than you do through listening.[55]

Using the research, let's say your son reads a Middle Grade/YA chapter book/novel. Reading this book will expose him to many more rare words than if he spends time listening to college graduates have a conversation or watches prime time television. By adding comic books to his reading mix, he'll be exposed to significantly more vocabulary words. Comic books actually have three times more rare words than a college graduate conversation, and provide almost double the exposure when compared to Middle Grade chapter books.

The more printed sources your son reads (chapter books, comic books, newspaper articles, biographies, etc.), the more pages he'll read, and the more vocabulary he'll be exposed to, learn and accumulate.

It's the accumulation process that makes the difference. The more your son reads what he enjoys every day, the more he will become exposed to rare words—often the *same* rare word, multiple times.

This is when vocabulary-building starts to take hold in earnest and there's a measurable return on reading investment.

Over time, cumulative reading actually makes you smarter, no matter what your early intellectual/cognitive ability was. The researchers also found that those who read a lot will boost their verbal intelligence by building their vocabulary and general knowledge, even if their earlier experiences showed otherwise. They emphatically state how imperative frequent pleasure reading (not foundational, standardized or mandatory) is for those who struggle with their comprehension skills and verbal abilities.[56]

Through cumulative reading and expanding his vocabulary, your son will eventually be ready to comprehend more complex printed texts, which will expose him to even more rare words, and so on and so forth. At the same time your son expands his understanding of words and their multiple meanings and nuances, he also builds extensive background knowledge, strengthens his thinking and reading skills, and exercises and strengthens his neural connections.

By *not* pleasure reading every day, he missed out on building the vocabulary, background knowledge and structures that are required to comprehend a complex text, and now he needs to hunker down and make up for lost time.

Because you balance... your son will strengthen his thinking and reading skills.

I'm going to share a story about two boys, using the reading frequency chart I shared earlier, the 2015 NAEP 8th grade boys' reading achievement results, and a visual I created, called the Reading Moves Ladder. First, I'm going to give you background information, to help you understand what I mean by thinking and reading skills. Then, when I tell the tale of the two boys, you will have a better grasp on what is happening in your son's head when he reads.

Every two years, NAEP releases a national report card on the state of reading in the United States. It's a sample of students and schools across the country, not a high-stakes test, and teachers can't prepare students for it. This assessment provides a snapshot of how the US is doing as a nation, not a single state, and is considered a trusted source of data. The 8th Grade Reading Moves Ladder I created shows how NAEP assesses the reading test and what their markers are to differentiate advanced, proficient and non-proficient readers.

Reading Performance and Frequency Chart			
Proficiency	8th Grade	Time Read/Day	Words Read/Yr
% Advanced Readers	2%	21.1 minutes	1,823,000
% Proficient	27%	14.2 minutes	1,146,000
% Non-Proficient	71%	6 seconds–9.6 minutes	8,000–622,000

Adapted from 2015 NAEP results[57]

The 8th Grade Reading Moves Ladder visually represents what thinking and stamina look like in the mind of an advanced, proficient and non-proficient 8th grade reader when they are expected to read 8th grade-level text. The reading cognitive targets (locate/recall, integrate/interpret and critique/evaluate) that NAEP measures work together like rungs on a ladder.[58] To make it to the top, it's critical to step on each rung, starting from the first one at the bottom. No one ever suggests running and leaping onto the middle rungs on a ladder to get to the top quicker, and it works the same with the reading cognitive targets.

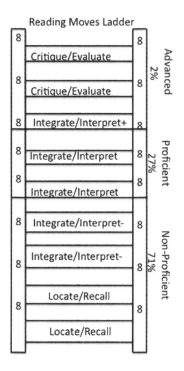

The bottom rungs—locate/recall—are the check-points for accurately reading details and facts that are explicitly stated in the text. Once a reader accurately grasps those details and facts, the next rungs check their *understanding* of the text. The integrate/interpret rungs now expect a reader to bring their own thinking to the text by inferring, making comparisons, and examining relationships of ideas across the text. The middle rungs progressively expect more sophisticated thinking and reasoning from the reader as they move closer to the critique/evaluate rungs at the top.

The top rungs require the reader to have read for accuracy and understood what they read, before they can think critically about the text and evaluate it. Without stamina, engagement, and success with the bottom and middle rungs, the critique/evaluate rungs are impossible to achieve. This is because they expect a reader to critically and thoughtfully examine a text from numerous perspectives, have deep familiarity with how texts are structured, and connect ideas cohesively across multiple texts.

When a boy reads a text, he doesn't just start at the first rung and move upward to the second rung in a lock-step manner. Reading is active and fluid. He constantly runs up and down the ladder, depending on the structure of the text, his background knowledge of the text, the complexity of the text, his understanding of the text, and his stamina, motivation and interest in the text.

Tale of Two Readers

8th Grade Advanced Reader (2% of boys): Imagine that this boy has read every day for 30 minutes since fourth grade. When he sat down to take the NAEP eighth-grade reading assessment, he had already read well over 7,300,000 words (1,823,000 words/ year x 4 years) and was exposed to a wide range of rare words, dramatically expanding his vocabulary, background knowledge and "smarts." Even though he didn't care about the assessment, he had brought a ton of reading experience to the table, and his brain put him on autopilot because of all of his practice, running up and down the ladder in his spare time. This meant he had plenty of stamina, dynamic neural connections to tap into numerous perspectives and structures, agility in his thinking to connect ideas across multiple texts, and a deep understanding of what he read because of the expansive vocabulary he had accumulated over the years.

8th Grade Non-Proficient Reader (71% of boys): Imagine that this boy had read hit or miss since fourth grade, so on average he read on the high end of non-proficiency, about 10 minutes a day. A majority of the time, his reading distractors took center stage, unless he was forced to read or a book he liked fell into his lap. By the time he sat down to take the NAEP eighth-grade test, he had only read approximately 2,500,000 words (622,000 words/ year x 4 years)—about the same amount that the advanced reader was exposed to in about 1½ years of his reading. By not pleasure reading every day, he missed many rare word opportunities to build an expansive vocabulary, and it eventually caught up with him. The eighth-grade reading material was too challenging, he didn't have the stamina or the neural connections needed to run up and down the ladder, and the passages made no sense to him because there were too many words that he didn't understand.

Here's where it's important to remember the definition of a rare word—a word outside the vocabulary of a 6th grader—and that the only way to actually learn seventh- and eighth-grade level vocabulary for the long term is by pleasure reading—a lot. No wonder the non-pleasure reading boy didn't have the necessary eighth-grade vocabulary to understand what he was reading. He wasn't exposed to it! Watching television, playing video games—or even a musical instrument or sports—couldn't expose him to rare words. Foundational and standardized reading couldn't expose him to them either, and his mandatory reading on grade-level texts is what gave him the only vocabulary that he has.

Now let's imagine that the eighth-grade non-proficient reader continues on this path. It's important to know that the Reading

Moves Ladder just keeps getting taller and more substantial with each grade (for example, the ninth-grade ladder will add a few more rungs). Even if he's not ready for the next Ladder, it doesn't matter; he still must turn in the current grade's Ladder at the end of the school year, and start with his new grade's Ladder in September.

Three years later, when he reaches 11th grade, it's time for him to take the new SAT. If he never included 30 minutes of daily pleasure reading into his schedule, how do you think he'll cope with 11th grade/college-ready vocabulary and text complexity on the day he takes the SAT?

Cramming and hoping won't help him be the best version of himself on the test, or in college and beyond.

Pleasure reading is one thing every boy can do for himself to have a huge return on investment for his long-term goals, dreams and future success. In a study that started in 1970, researchers found that those who were successful at 42 years of age were the same kids who had read for pleasure at 10 and 16 years of age.[59] This group had a more extensive vocabulary than those who hadn't read in their spare time. They also had better math and spelling skills, which continued into adulthood.

Reading every day matters, and so does what is read. The same adults who read frequently as kids and scored high on the vocabulary tests given at ages 10 and 16, were now reading literary and classic fiction, plus the newspaper every day. This group graduated from elite universities, worked in professional jobs, and had the highest vocabulary scores, compared to the adults who hadn't read as kids and who had scored low on their vocabulary tests.

The study concluded that an extensive vocabulary is what makes professional attainment possible, and pleasure reading during childhood is the single best way to accumulate the level of vocabulary needed.

It's important to note that this research also found that pleasure reading in childhood matters more for a person's future success than their parents' education levels and socio-economic status. If a boy lives with educated parents who are wealthy, this alone doesn't ensure success if he doesn't choose to read for pleasure every day. On the other hand, if a boy lives with high-school graduates who are struggling financially but he reads for pleasure every day, because he *is* reading, he's also giving himself a chance for a more successful future than his parents. [60]

Both of my parents had only graduated from high school and struggled financially throughout my childhood. Even so, my brother and I read for pleasure all of the time, and it's why we are successful today. The act of reading on our own gave us hope, vocabulary and background knowledge, and the opportunity to be the best versions of ourselves. My brother is a college graduate and an executive in an advertising agency, and I taught for more than 20 years and obtained a master's degree from an Ivy League university. Neither of us struggle financially, we both continue to read every day, and my brother's children (a boy and girl) are both voracious readers.

Reading distractors must be balanced with pleasure reading because it is the only activity/habit/hobby/interest or type of reading that will develop your son's vocabulary.

Practice makes permanent.

What is your son practicing?

The best time to plant a tree was 20 years ago. The second best time is now."—Chinese Proverb

ACTION STEPS

1. Tough Question: Do you help balance your son's visible and invisible reading distractors (competing demands, technology/media, homework, standardized testing, stereotyping and multi-tasking)? All, some, none? Which ones do you balance and how?

Time is precious, and your son's time is especially precious to him. Because of this, to him the idea of balancing his time will seem as if you're taking away the air he breathes and he'll die without it. To him, pleasure reading will be a *cost* in his life, not a benefit. This is his amygdala (the brain's emotional center) reacting. Instead of becoming frustrated and wanting to give in and give up (something you may have done in the past), think of it as follows: Your son's brain is brilliantly doing its job, and now it's time for *your* frontal lobe—the decision-making center—to brilliantly take over. Neutralizing the situation by appreciating how your brains work differently and moving forward from there, diminishes the reactive nature of the amygdala for both of you.

2. Determining Your Son's Reading Distractors, the Time Spent on Them, and His Hot Button Distractor(s): Understanding your son's distractors is key, but going one step further and figuring out the hot button distractor(s) (those that are emotionally highly charged for your son) will make all the difference later. OLBE will help you to think and plan ahead.

- **Observe:** Watching your son do what comes naturally is the most effective way to gain knowledge about his distractors. When you *observe*, it's not the time to interfere or correct or punish; it's the time to pay attention to how your son approaches, embraces and utilizes his spare time. Do specific competing demands take up much of his after-school schedule, or is it technology/media? How does he complete his homework? In one sitting, or does he procrastinate? Does he say worrisome things about standardized test prep and testing or about himself and others as readers? Is your son multitasking? Spend a few days really seeing, hearing, and feeling what your son is doing and saying.

- **List:** Fill in the following chart with what you have learned about your son's distractors. Try to capture as much as possible about each one without judging them.

6 Common Reading Distractors	Your son's distractors	Approximate Time Spent
Competing Demands		
Homework		
Technology/Media		
Standardized Testing		
Stereotyping		
Multitasking		

- **Brainstorm:** Re-read your notes from the chart above and pay attention to those you would consider his hot buttons. Maybe it's the intensity in his eyes, the excitement in his voice giving you the clue, or the cursing under his breath whenever it's time to do his social studies homework. Or it can be the visceral reaction he had to being called a reader or the stomach ache he had at breakfast on the day his class practiced for the reading standardized test. You know your son best, so once you intentionally focus on the distractors, his hot button distractor(s) will start to stand out loud and clear.

- **Explore**: Figuring out where and how to add 30 minutes of reading to your son's schedule is both a necessary and a daunting task. Because you're your son's frontal lobe during this process, he needs you to do it for him, yet he's old enough to not want your help and has no problem letting you know it!

Here's some good news: just like starting a new exercise program, it's not suggested to dive right into 30 minutes a day of reading if your son has never read or hasn't read a book in a long time. Like physical stamina, cognitive stamina takes time to build, and you don't want to burn your son out before he's had a chance to really begin. With only 10 minutes a day of pleasure reading, research shows a 1429% increase in word exposure (and therefore more rare words) at the end of one year.[61] It's also the difference between being on the bottom rung of the Reading Moves Ladder or on the rung right below proficiency. This alleviates the pressure of trying to re-allocate 30 minutes in your son's day.

Choose the amount of time you think makes the most sense for your son to balance his distractors in the beginning: 10, 15, 20, 25 or 30 minutes a day of pleasure reading. As things progress, you will add five minutes, but at the beginning of the process, even 10 minutes works.

Next, use your brainstorm list to determine the hot button distractors you shouldn't touch right now.* For example: an obsession with a video game, watching a certain set of TV shows, hanging out with his friends, or his soccer coach taking up all his spare time. Working around those, explore possible times in his day where pleasure reading might work and for how long. Try to find at least five different possibilities that you can write down and use in Building Block 9: Pinpoint.

*Transforming the non-reading habit to the reading habit is difficult enough on its own. To then take away or try to address his highly-charged emotional distractors doesn't make sense right now. I suggest keeping the hot button distractor(s) intact for the time being. It needs to be one or the other. If you feel the hot button distractor reveals itself to be the more immediate issue, I suggest putting the reading habit on hold and first devote your effort toward dealing with the distractor. As I stated earlier, you know your son best and will know what is the most appropriate course of action to take.

KEY TAKEAWAYS... Building Block 7: Balance

- There are six common reading distractors boys need to balance: competing demands; homework; technology/media; standardized testing; stereotyping; and multitasking, so that his developing adolescent brain exercises and strengthens neural connections that are only made by reading.
- 30 minutes a day of pleasure reading is the sweet spot to gain all of its benefits.
- It's important to understand why your son will see reading as a cost instead of a benefit.
- Pleasure reading is the only way your son will develop the type of expansive long-term vocabulary that is needed for success.
- Pleasure reading—not foundational, standardized or mandatory reading—strengthens thinking and reading skills.

Balancing your son's distractor(s) with reading helps you zero in on how he is using his time. In Building Block 8: Adjust, you will now step back and see the big picture of where your son is standing.

Visit the following link to download the vocabulary analogy I created for you.

This analogy is an example of how I explained the return on investment of vocabulary development to preteen and early teen boys so they understood what they were "leaving on the table" when they chose to not read for pleasure.

http://www.hillarytubin.com/freevocabanalogy

❧ BUILDING BLOCK 8: ADJUST ❧

Your son needs you to adjust his schedule according to the time of year, his competing demands, and your expectations, as determined by his brain/age/grade (BAG) developmental needs.

THE RIPPLE EFFECTS OF ADJUSTING

Because you adjust... your son's pleasure reading schedule will be tailored to the seasons and his competing demands.

Pleasure reading schedules must be firmly established, yet flexible. Non-negotiable, yet fluid. Once they are developed, they are not set in stone, to just leave and forget. Instead, think of your son's pleasure reading plan as a living, breathing document that requires ongoing attention from both of you. It has to adapt and adjust to changing conditions so it can persist through them all.

Your son must read every day to gain the benefits of pleasure reading (firmly established and non-negotiable), yet when, where and how he does this needs to be determined according to the seasons (flexible and fluid). Because of this, your ability to adjust and show your son how to adapt is critical to instilling the reading habit. Building blocks 1–7 analyzed why it's not optional for your son to read for pleasure every day, and *this* building block explains why taking the reality of life into consideration isn't optional, either.

Different seasons require different things from your family and your son. The more you know and understand your calendar and his calendar up front, the easier it is to plan ahead and make the necessary adjustments before it's too late. By too late, I mean that if your son stops reading for 30 minutes a day because his schedule and the demands on him change and he becomes too busy and overwhelmed, this becomes an excuse to stop his reading routine altogether and then you'll have an uphill battle on your hands to re-instate it.

What I share here is my experience as a literacy educator, working with preteen/early teen boys and their families on the reading habit through 20 seasonal cycles. I discovered that each season brings its pros (for reading to flourish) or cons (for it to wither), depending on the degree of planning that was done ahead of time.

Because I taught the same boys for three years, I learned that no matter the season, self-proclaimed non-reading sixth-grade boys required a lot of adult support, involvement and adjustment for their reading to flourish. On the other hand, if this initial investment was thoughtfully and purposefully put into place, it later created a huge return on that investment. I found that, once boys lived through each season's adjustments one time, by eighth grade, they actually adjusted their reading habit routine on their own.

Most likely your son is also a self-proclaimed non-reader. This means that—whether he's 9 or 14 years old—in the beginning he, too, needs you to adjust his schedule and to support, guide, and model the adjustments, so he can learn how to do it for himself.

To help you think about your seasons and schedule, I'm going to share what it looks like on the East Coast of the United States. Here we have four distinct seasons, and many of the states' schools and sports follow similar schedules. Your state or country has its own distinct seasons and schedules, so it's important that you adapt and modify what I describe to fit with the patterns in your own area.

Fall

For most boys, it was difficult to acclimate to being back indoors and burdened with structures and expectations. They needed time to adjust and work back into regular routines after the more flexible summer months. It typically took most boys about one month to get back into the groove of doing homework and being in school. Boys who also played a sport needed even more support to stay on track and not fall behind. Many were secretly stressed about staying organized and fitting everything in, and when they couldn't do that, school work and homework were the first things to go.

September is not the best month to instill the reading habit in your son. It's a great month for you to model reading for him, but not for him to try to include reading for pleasure in his day.

Starting in October, I expected boys (with the help of their parents) to find 10 minutes in their schedule to read for pleasure, 7 days a week. Some read in the morning before school, some before going to bed, others right after school (before doing any other homework), and others listened to books in the car on their way to and from an activity. Due to varied schedules each day, some read at different times on different days. As long as the boys fully grasped that reading for pleasure was non-negotiable, and they had a system to remember the time (an alarm on their phone, a calendar hanging on the refrigerator, etc.), I could live with it.

One date in October stood out: Halloween always distracted boys. The thought of free candy and dressing up as a   (fill in the blank) typically kept them preoccupied for one week beforehand and a few days after, but pleasure reading for 10 minutes a day remained non-negotiable, even on Halloween.

In my experience, the entire month of November up to mid-December was when boys finally felt comfortable with their schedules and routines and were ready to learn. This is when I ramped up their reading time from 10 minutes to 30 minutes. They needed to discuss with their parents how to adjust their schedules to add 20 more minutes of pleasure reading to their day. Some ended up adding only 5 or 10 more minutes, depending on competing demands like sports or extra music rehearsals/practice for holiday concerts, but as long as they read, this worked.

Winter

In mid-December, during the two weeks leading up to winter break and the holidays right up to the day before vacation begins, boys are excited and distracted in school and in life. By this point, because most boys now had the reading habit and a set schedule in place, they continued to read each day on autopilot, without reminders. I also expected them to read every day during winter break, and this meant they had to adjust their schedule and make sure they remembered to read. In my last years of teaching, many boys ended up getting an e-reader and gift cards for books as gifts, which made reading during their vacation a lot more fun.

For boys who did not have the reading habit in place, this was not the time to push to make it happen.

On the other hand, January and February were what I called

"learning nirvana" for boys. They came back from winter break ready to go. Being in the swing of things, they felt more comfortable with their routines; competing demands created less stress in their lives, opening them up to new things. Limiting their video-game playing or TV-watching to include pleasure reading no longer felt like a loss or a cost to them, and their parents were now able to legitimately take the back seat. After three months of being in the driver's seat—believing, investing, modeling, walking and talking, appreciating, prioritizing, balancing and adjusting— their sons were able to take the wheel themselves and be in charge of their reading for pleasure, without as much adult supervision.

For a few boys, everything I taught them happened in January and February, including the reading habit. I found that, with any boys who still struggled with consistently reading for pleasure, this was the best time to hunker down with them and make it happen.

One, they were ready. And two, it gave them at least two months of critical pleasure reading under their belt before standardized reading took over from mid-March to mid-April, and the craziness of trying to adapt to a spring schedule began.

Spring

I learned that March, April and May were the worst months to transform a boy's non-reading habit into the reading habit. Between standardized testing, an upswing in socializing that came with the nicer weather and it being light later, spring sports/ activities starting, and the combination of grade-level academic expectations (foundational and mandatory reading) amping up at the same time the school year was winding down, reading distractors increase tremendously.

If a boy's reading habit wasn't in place by spring, April and May (like September and the time heading into winter break) were not the months to push him.

Boys with the reading habit in place only needed to adjust their winter reading schedule to accommodate the abundance of activity and disruptions that are typical in spring. Their parents were available for support and guidance, but by mid-April, most boys could adjust their own schedules. I also only expected them to pleasure read for 10 minutes a day during the last two months of school. Much of the time, many still read for 30 minutes (on top of their mandatory reading), but knowing that they only had to find room in their schedule for 10 minutes of reading for pleasure eliminated a lot of added stress.

Summer

Some school districts close down after Memorial Day, and others stay open into June. Fortunately, I had the first two weeks in June to prepare my students for pleasure reading during the rest of June, July and August.

Summer break is both a blessing and a curse for boys. It brings the freedom they crave; however, it also means the absence of the structures and routines they need to guide them in how they use their time. Then there's the required summer reading that most boys have "hanging over their head" (this was how boys typically described it to me). Because mandatory reading is equated with pain, I found boys typically handled summer reading in two different ways: the "get it over with" method or the "put it off until the last possible moment" method, and sometimes their moms jumped in for yet a third way.

The "get it over with" method is when boys read the required book(s) and do the assignment(s) right after school lets out and then don't pick up another book until school begins again. Many would share how awesome it made the rest of their summer, knowing that everything was done and in their backpack for the first day of school.

The "put it off until the last possible moment" method is when— the minute school lets out—boys forget they even *have* required reading. Anywhere from one week before school starts, to one day or even *one hour* before the assignment is due, it all comes rushing back to them that something is due on the first day of school. They skim, scan and cram the required book(s) in no time, and then throw together something about anything that's supposed to resemble the assignment.

The "mom jumps in" method is when a boy's mom knows about the assignment and is tired of nagging. There are two versions of this method. Version 1 is when a mom (sometimes with her son by her side, or on her own) quickly reads the book(s) and completes the assignment(s) for her son (either by holding the pencil herself or telling her son what he needs to write). Version 2 is when a mom keeps her son from all activities for as long as it takes him to read the books and do the assignments, usually sitting at the kitchen or dining room table, so she can watch him and his progress.

All three of these methods are problematic and harmful for boys, especially boys who are struggling with reading.

Summer Reading Loss

Summer reading loss is a real problem, not only because it makes September much more difficult, but the decline in reading achievement and the vocabulary loss each summer are cumulative. Every summer that a boy doesn't read for pleasure each day, his losses compound and can't be recouped until he begins to read for pleasure again.

To explain, I want you to imagine two sixth-grade boys who ended the school year with identical reading levels (one year behind grade level) and identical scores on a reading achievement assessment (Basic).

Boy A's mom decided summer vacation was a great time to get her son to read for pleasure. She had some ideas for books and topics he might want to learn about, and tons of ideas for cool reading spots and reading field trips they could take together, now that she was reading, too. The librarian at the public library recommended other books for boys and showed her how to access electronic books from her home computer, using the online library. She then found a used Kindle for her son and showed him how to navigate the online library to choose and take out books.

Over the summer, Boy A read for 30 minutes every day after he came home from basketball camp and before he went to play soccer with his friends in the park. Some days he read even more because he loved reading books on his Kindle, chilling under a tree in his backyard. He played his video games at night. He included his summer reading books in his daily 30-minute reading and he did the required assignments (without being reminded) before school started. Because he had read the books, the assignments were actually fun and easy. By the time September rolled around, he had read about 350,000 words and was really looking forward to seventh grade.

Boy B threw his backpack in the closet on the last day of school and didn't take it out until vacation was over. In *his* home, there was no talk about books or reading, so he didn't even think about it. Every day after basketball camp, he played soccer at the park with his friends. At night he played his video games. Right before school started, his friend (Boy A) reminded him of the summer reading books and the assignments that were due on the first day of school. Boy B found his backpack and books, quickly skimmed them, threw together something to hand in to the teacher, crossed his fingers, and hoped she wouldn't really look at the assignment. By the time school started, he had read less than 1,000 words and kept getting a stomach ache whenever he thought about seventh grade.

The difference between the two boys boiled down to 30 minutes a day of reading for pleasure, but what a difference that made!

Research has found that kids who had easy access to books over the summer read more, and by reading a minimum of four or five books during that time, they prevented a decline in reading achievement scores from the spring to the fall.[62] Another study concluded that the one summer activity that is consistently related to academic gains is reading. Not vacation trips and participation in organized activities like sports or camp, but frequently reading books or regularly visiting the library.[63]

My experience confirms the research. Boy A and Boy B are real examples of boys going into the summer before seventh grade each year; just change the specific activities they engage with to those that your son engages with and see what that means for him. On the first day of school, it was easy to figure out who had read for 30 minutes every day and who hadn't. Because Boy A read for pleasure throughout June, July and August, he started seventh grade reading on a seventh-grade level. I found that boys who were reading below grade level when they left school for the summer, but read for pleasure every day *during* the summer, consistently returned to school in September *on* grade level (or even above grade level) and never looked back.

On a sad note, by not reading that summer, Boy B never caught up to Boy A academically, once the gap had occurred. When Boy B started seventh grade in September, it took him time to acclimate to school, so he missed out on even more vocabulary building and strengthening of his reading cognitive skills. By the time he got himself together to read for pleasure in November, Boy A had already read another 350,000 words (700,000 words in total), compared to Boy B's 1,000 words (2,000 words total).

Use summer to your advantage. It is the best season to transform the non-reading habit into the reading habit with your son. By doing so, your son will be fully ready for the next grade, and will have momentum in September to keep reading and learning. Now he won't fall further behind or feel stressed, because pleasure reading is the antidote to *underperformance disease.*

As long as you help your son adjust his pleasure reading schedule to fit with his seasonal demands, he'll finally have a way to get off the underperformance hamster wheel and will begin to see results he can feel good about.

Because you adjust... you will understand your son's developmental BAG needs and keep them front and center when you form your own expectations for him.

Besides the seasons and your son's competing demands, it's also important to consider his brain/age/and grade needs (BAG) from 9–14-years of age. With each passing year and season, your son's cognitive, emotional and social needs shift and develop (his physical needs change, too, but I'm not going to focus on them in this book), and *you* need to adjust with them. If not, trying to instill the reading habit in your preteen/early teen son quickly becomes a tension-filled, hair-pulling nightmare, making it difficult for you to not want to give up entirely.

The more you can wrap your head around his current BAG needs, the better you'll position yourself to know what to expect and not take what your son dishes out too personally. It's also important to know ahead of time that change is swift during adolescence and, just as soon as you think you have a handle on who your son is, whoosh! It changes again. Be willing and able to adjust.

Just as you were getting comfortable with your fifth-grade son's bug collection taking over the dining room, he's over it and on to something new. Except he didn't tell you, because now he spends most of his time in his room whispering to someone on the phone. It makes your head spin.

That's why it's critical to know exactly where your son stands developmentally before you instill the reading habit in him. Think about it: helping your fifth-grade son (the bug collector) to include reading in his life is a very different undertaking than helping your reclusive 12-year-old son, (who now only wears black and whispers on the phone) to include reading in *his* life. Each version of your son will need something completely different from you to instill the reading habit, and it's only through your continuous adjustments to the changes he is going through that you can make sure you meet your son where he *is*.

Awareness and knowledge of the key developmental charac-teristics typical of boys ages 9–11 and boys ages 12–14 puts perspective on your son's current cognitive, emotional and social development. It also helps you navigate the best ways to help your son develop his reading habit during this uncertain, wobbly time. When you're mindful and understanding of how he sees himself, you, his friends and the world, you're more open, able, inspired and confident, because *you* are prepared.

When you're unaware of your son's current developmental stage, frustration (and even anger) may fill your conversations with him and this won't help. Remember that he *needs* you to be the frontal brain that he lacks during this time.

In Building Block 7: Balance, you learned how your son's brain is currently developing its frontal part (the decision-making, planning and organizing part) and while it's under construction, you'll share yours with him. This is because—without his thinking part working properly yet—your son will respond with his amygdala (the emotional part of his brain) instead. Without you there to exercise and activate the neural connections in his frontal lobe and influence and inspire his future success, it won't happen on its own.

When you then add the cognitive, emotional and social developmental changes your son will experience at the same time that his brain is developing, things about your son begin to make more sense.

Below are a few examples that compare the common characteristics of a 9- to 11-year-old boy with those of a 12- to 14-year-old boy. You'll start to notice the differences between the two age groups. Sixth grade falls in both categories, because many boys start the year in one group and end the year in another, because age and grade don't always line up in a nice neat way.

Cognitive Development*

Thinking Capacity of 9- to 11-year-old Boys (4th–6th grade)
- They think in terms of what is tangible, real and concrete (literal thinking).
- They judge ideas in absolutes (right or wrong), with not much tolerance for the middle ground.
- They are able to learn to use good judgment.

Thinking Capacity of 12- to 14-year-old Boys (6th- 8th grade)
- They have more capacity for complex thinking.
- Their thinking is becoming more abstract, with better reasoning and more intellectual curiosity.
- They are able to think logically and to think about thinking (metacognition).
- They understand metaphors, double meanings and more sophisticated humor (nuances in language).

Impact of Thinking Capacity on Instilling the Reading Habit

When presenting the idea of reading for pleasure, the younger your son is, the more tangible and concrete you'll need to be with why reading for fun is important. Older boys can handle a more complex argument, as long as compelling reasons and evidence are thoughtfully explained and shared.

Emotional Development*

How Authority Is Viewed by 9- to 11-year-old Boys (4th-6th grade)
- They see adults as authority, but begin to test/question to see what's negotiable.
- They need/want emotional support/involvement/encourage- ment from parents/caring adults.

- They do things to avoid punishment.
- They begin to question rules and beliefs that they previously took at face value.

How Authority Is Viewed by 12- to 14-year-old Boys (6ᵗʰ-8ᵗʰ grade)
- They continue to test rules and limits and begin to question social conventions.
- They blatantly reject parental standards.
- They express less affection towards parents; they sometimes seem rude and short-tempered.
- They become critical and argumentative, yet overreact to parental questions and criticisms.

The Impact of How Authority Is Viewed on Instilling the Reading Habit

Boys are paying attention to what you do and say, and it's their job right now to call you out on the things that don't add up. They're going to test your mettle with your own reading, which is why—before anything else—*you* must become the reader that you want your son to be.

Social Development*

Influence of Peers on 9- to 11-year-old Boys (4ᵗʰ–6ᵗʰ grade)
- Their group identity and time with friends is important; they're loyal to groups, clubs, etc.
- They start forming stronger, more complex friendships and peer relationships.
- Having same-gender friends is very important; they identify more with individuals of the same gender.
- They begin to feel peer pressure.
- They have a first crush or are pressured to have a crush.

Influence of Peers on 12- to 14-year-old Boys (6th–8th grade)
- They identify with their peer group.
- They rely on their peer group for support.
- Their conformity and not being different from peers is very important because social status and acceptance depends on conformity to observable traits or roles.
- They experience peer pressure to use alcohol, tobacco, drugs, and engage in sexual activities.
- Short-term romantic relationships may occur.
- "Showing off" may increase.

Influence of Parents/Others on 9- to 11-year-old Boys
- **They accept/rely on parental guidance but also seek more independence.**

Influence of Parents/Others on 12- to 14-year-old Boys
- They assert their independence, but feel conflicted because they continue to find/crave safety and security in the structures and limits set by parents and others.
- They psychologically distance themselves from parents/demand distance from parents, but often want close relationships with other adults outside of the family.
- They see themselves differently when they are with their peers, compared to how they see themselves when they are with parents and teachers.
- They have a greater need for privacy and time alone in the house.
- **They seek acceptance from peers, but still look to parents for values and guidance.**
- **Adult role models are important.**

*Adapted from American Academy of Pediatrics (healthychildren.org) [64] and *The Teen Years Explained* (McNeely and Blanchard)[65]

"Parents and caring adults often underestimate their capacity to promote young people's development. Because of their developmental stage, young people stop letting adults know that they are important in the young people's worlds, or, for that matter, that the adults even matter. But teens consistently report, and research confirms, that adults remain essential care-givers, role models, educators, and mentors."—The Teen Years Explained

The above information makes it clear why instilling the reading habit in your son earlier in his life may be less difficult than waiting until he's 12, 13, or 14 years old, but with awareness, knowledge and a mindful plan that is determined by your son's BAG needs, it shouldn't matter how old he is. What matters is whether he continues to *not* read for pleasure.

If your son is 12, 13 or 14 years old, this is his chance to develop his vocabulary and invest in his future before he sits for the SATs and heads out into the world on his own. Remember the Reading Moves Ladder in Building Block 7: Balance. Reading skills and vocabulary won't wait for your son to catch up. They become more sophisticated and nuanced, and the texts become more complex as your son moves up from grade to grade. However, if he reads for pleasure every day and also reads his mandatory reading throughout high school, he'll be ready to handle the College- and Knowledge-Based-Economy-Ready Ladder.

Using the earlier example comparing Boy A and Boy B during the summer, I want to explain what I mean by "reading skills and vocabulary won't wait for your son to catch up."

When Boy A and Boy B both ended sixth grade, they were only able to run up and down the fifth-grade Reading Moves Ladder.

The sixth-grade Ladder made them so mentally exhausted, they couldn't get past the bottom rungs, even at the end of the year.

When Boy A returned to school in September, because his mother had adjusted and figured out what her 12-year-old son would need to read (a Kindle and easy access to getting books on his Kindle), his reading achievement improved. He could now run up and down the sixth-grade Ladder without getting tired and was ready for the seventh-grade Ladder.

When Boy B returned to school in September, because he didn't read at all over the summer, he stayed on the fifth-grade Ladder, but he no longer could even make it to the top rungs. Even so, he is still given the seventh-grade Ladder and he will be tested on it at the end of the year. The system assumes he is ready, when he is not.

There's still a chance for Boy B. He has plenty of time before high school to transform his reading habit. He just needs modeling, guidance, support and the help of an adult's frontal lobe and willingness to adjust to figure out how.

ACTION STEPS

1. Tough Question: Do you adjust your son's schedule according to the time of year and his competing demands, coupled with adjusting your expectations/approach, based on his brain/age/ grade (BAG) needs?

Whether *you* adjust is what determines the success of your son's reading habit transformation. Without your adjusting, the entire foundation crumbles. In my experience, this is where some parents of boys became stuck. They couldn't or wouldn't wrap their heads around the power of timing and the brain, age and grade development research. Instead, if their son didn't read *what* they wanted and/or expected, *when* they wanted it and/or expected it, they placed blame on individual people, institutions or systems. To them, "adjusting" meant lowering their expectations or giving in to their son's wants—not taking into account their BAG needs— and they couldn't or wouldn't do it.

In theory, they appreciated that certain boys needed to read comic books, graphic novels or skate-boarding magazines—just not *their* son. In theory, it made sense that preteens/early teens needed independence from their parents, questioned their beliefs and tested limits—just not *their* son. Many parents weren't ready to let go of the little boy they were able to mold and shape just because they were the parent. This made it very difficult for them to instill, transform and nurture the reading habit the way I have suggested, so they fought it.

At this juncture, the difference between boys whose parents adjusted and boys whose parents didn't was very obvious. Those who adjusted had sons who not only read every day, but also loved to read and talk to their parents about what they read. These parents would tell me over and over again how much they enjoyed their son and how interesting he had become. The non-adjusting parents' sons did fine with foundational, standardized and mandatory reading, but because pleasure reading caused pain, they didn't grow in critical ways to become the best versions of themselves.

2. Decide the best time of the year to instill your son's reading habit: At minimum, it will take 90 consecutive days for your son to transform his non-reading habit into the reading habit. Some seasons are better suited for this level of intense work than other seasons. Starting sooner, rather than later, is important, but not if "sooner" has a lot of disruptions, stress, and/or competing demands, and if it doesn't give *you* enough time to first become the reading model your son needs you to be for him.

Adjusting your son's schedule so that pleasure reading happens every day is his key to success. However, thinking ahead and planning for the time of year his schedule has the least distractions will make adjusting less necessary for both of you.

In my experience, the three best times of the year to instill the reading habit in your son are **early January, early June, and early October.** Not that other times won't work, but I was most successful when I waited until the first school day in January, June or October to meet and plan with boys.

My second book will provide details about each phase of the 90 days. However, for planning purposes, it's important to know what level of support each phase requires from you.

Phase 1, Initiate: 30 Days (January, June, or October)
The first 30 days is when your son needs your support, belief and frontal lobe the most. Your role during this month is very hands-on. When determining your possible start dates, think about *your* calendar, as well as your son's. For example, if the month of October into early November is when you are the busiest at work and will be home late more nights than not, this is not a good time to begin. However, if things are calmest in January, wait until then to meet with your son, and while you're waiting, make sure to spend the time reading and talking to him about what you're reading.

Phase 2, Transform: 30 Days (February, July, or November)
During the second 30 days, you are still needed, but your role

is more hands-off than hands-on. This is when you're gradually releasing the reading habit responsibilities to your son. He won't be great at first, but by the end of the month a huge transformation takes place, hence the name of the phase. During this phase, you need to be available and continue as your son's reading model, but you'll be in the background. Think of it like your son now has his learner's permit and has taken over the wheel, but you must still be in the car.

Phase 3, Nurture: 30 Days (March, August, or December)
If your son has read consecutively for 60 days, this phase is to ensure the reading habit is firmly in place. Your role is mostly hands-off and just making yourself available if your son needs you. Imagine that your son just got his driver's license and it's the first month he is driving without you in the car. You still will remind him of things before he drives off and ask him questions about how it went when he returns. But with each day you trust more and begin to release the responsibility of his driving onto him. It's the same thing with the reading habit, but way less scary.

In a notebook or the workbook, use the information about the seasons, your son's current schedule and competing demands, and your current schedule and competing demands, and write down the pros and cons of instilling in each of the seasons.

Winter (January, February, March):
Summer (June, July, August):
Fall (October, November, December):

From your notes, write down the season best suited for you and your son, and the date you are planning to instill the reading habit in your son (Saturday and Sunday are the best start dates).

Using a calendar, count how many days from today you have before meeting with your son.

Building Block 9: Pinpoint and Building Block 10: Plan are structured to insure that you will be fully prepared to meet and instill the reading habit in your son.

3. Before you meet with your son, adjust your expectations and approach by becoming aware of and knowledgeable about his current BAG needs: Now that you have an idea of when it's best to instill your son's reading habit, it's now time to think about his brain, age and grade needs and when you plan to begin. This information will be critical for your planning purposes in Building Block 10, Plan.

Answer the BAG questions below in a notebook or workbook.

BRAIN

- How old is your son today?
- How old will he be when you plan to initiate the reading habit with him?
- Re-read the Cognitive Development section that describes common characteristics of a boy your son's age. In a notebook or workbook, jot down the characteristics that most closely describe your son as he is right now, and how this will help you adjust your expectations and approach when planning. If your son is 11 or 12 years old, make sure to read both age categories.

Developmental Needs	Your son today	Adjusting Notes
Cognitive		

AGE

- Re-read the Emotional and Social Development sections that describe common characteristics of a boy your son's age. In a notebook or workbook, jot down the characteristics that most closely describe your son right now and how this will help you adjust your expectations and approach when planning. If your son is 11 or 12 years old, make sure to read both age categories.

Developmental Needs	Your son today	Adjusting Notes
Emotional		
Social		

GRADE

- What grade is your son in today?
- How would you describe your son's reading frequency?

Frequent reader: pleasure reads for 30 minutes, 5–7 days a week, in addition to the foundational, standardized and mandatory reading in and for school

Moderate reader: pleasure reads a couple times a month; typically reads when he likes something, but then won't read for a while outside of the foundational, standardized and mandatory reading in and for school

Infrequent reader: pleasure reads a couple times a year or not at all, outside of the foundational, standardized and mandatory reading in and for school.

To have a sense of how grade-level reading expectations bump up against your son's reading frequency, I placed a fourth-grade

Reading Moves Ladder next to the eighth-grade Ladder so you can visually see the difference.

Every year your son's new Ladder builds off of the previous grade's Ladder, becoming more complex, nuanced and taller, and new rungs are added. To reach the top of your son's grade-level Ladder by the end of the year, he needs to read over 1,823,000 words during the school year. If pleasure reading isn't a part of his life, that simply won't happen.

You want your son to be able to reach the critique/evaluate rung, even if it's not in a grade-level text at first. If your son never reads and is in sixth grade, he'll need to practice thinking while he reads books of interest to him, and they may be easy books. This is where you'll need to adjust your expectations by visualizing his grade-level Ladder and realizing that this Ladder is too much for him as he is right now. A smaller Ladder where he can run up and down it to exercise his brain will give him a taste of the benefits that reading offers him. As he keeps at it, like Boy A, your son will be ready for more complexity and the next Ladder in his pleasure reading.

Remember, pleasure reading is the keystone for all the other reading. Without it, your son will continue to sit at the bottom of each grade-level Ladder, always moving horizontally but never vertically.

KEY TAKEAWAYS... Building Block 8: Adjust

- Pleasure reading needs to be a non-negotiable part of your son's schedule every day. To do that, it's critical to think ahead so you can adjust for any competing demands that may arise.
- When determining the best time of year to instill your son's reading habit, find a 90-day window with minimal competing demands and the minimum need to adjust.

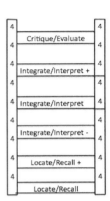
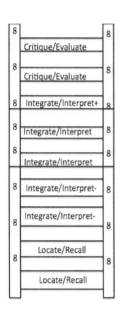

- Knowing your son's BAG needs (brain/age/grade), you will be able to adjust your expectations and approach so you meet him where he currently is, not where you think, want or hope he is.

Your willingness to adjust and meet your son where he is must be firmly in place before exploring his non-reading habit loop in Building Block 9: Pinpoint. That's because this block is when you are going to need to pay close attention to what makes your son tick, and the more aware and knowledgeable you are about his BAG needs, the easier it will be to do that.

Visit the following link to download the expanded CES (cognitive, emotional and social) Development chart I created for you.

This chart provides additional information about preteen and early teen boys' BAG needs and their impact when instilling the reading habit.

http://www.hillarytubin.com/freeCESchart

❧ BUILDING BLOCK 9: PINPOINT ❧

Your son needs you to pinpoint his non-reading habit loop (cue, routine, and reward) and then help him to transform it.

THE RIPPLE EFFECTS OF PINPOINTING

For Building Block 9: Pinpoint, I adapted Charles Duhigg's research and insights on habit formation from his book, *The Power of Habit* (2012).[66]

Because you pinpoint… you will understand how your son's non-reading habit formed.

A habit is typically an unconscious pattern of behavior that is acquired through frequent repetition, and this unconscious pattern of behavior can form in only two ways. According to Charles Duhigg, the two ways habits form are either through *unintentional* frequent repetition or *intentionally and deliberately designed* frequent repetition.

Because your son's non-reading habit formed through unintentional frequent repetition, it's important to first understand how this unintentional habit became automatic.

1) Left to its own devices, the brain really prefers not to work hard or exert effort unless someone on the outside intervenes on its behalf.
2) Because of this, without your son's knowledge, his brain constantly searched for ways to save effort after a long day of

school and homework filled with foundational, standardized and mandatory reading that caused him pain.

3) So when your son did things like play video games or watch TV or listen to music or talk on the phone for pleasure and relaxing, his brain said, "Ding ding ding ding ding," because it loved how non-taxing the activity was after a taxing day. This is the moment his brain grabbed onto the effort-saving opportunity and held on tight, hoping this activity would keep happening without someone intervening.

4) And it did. Every day, your son came home from school and repeated the same pleasure-producing activity. This is when his brain happily kicked into its favorite form of saving effort: automatic, non-thinking mode.

5) Once this happened repeatedly, your son's after school non-reading habit was unintentionally formed.

The good news: your son's *unintentional* non-reading habit can be transformed to become the *intentional* 30-minute-a-day reading habit.

The challenging news: It takes *your* frontal lobe, support, guidance, modeling and intervention to wake up your son's brain and move it out of its automatic, no-effort, non-reading mode into transformation mode.

Because you pinpoint... you'll know how to support your son's reading transformation.

The process your son needs to work through to transform his unintentional non-reading habit to the intentional reading habit is the exact same process a person must go through to transform their smoking habit to the non-smoking habit or their drinking habit to the non-drinking habit or their non-exercise habit to the exercise habit.

All habits, beneficial or harmful, are the same to the brain. It can't discern good or bad. All the brain understands is "effort" or "no effort." This is why it is difficult to rid ourselves of bad habits once they are on autopilot, and why the longer the habit is on autopilot, the harder it is to break.

Because of this, the goal of intentional and deliberate transformation is to get your son's brain to accept that the new, "good" habit can also become effortless and pleasurable. That's why snapping your fingers or hoping or demanding or punishing your son to make him read books can't ever work. There's no way for your son's brain to believe pleasure reading is really better than playing video games or watching TV or listening to music or talking on the phone for pleasure and relaxation.

Brains are smart like that. Remember, left to its own devices, your son's brain really prefers not to work hard or exert effort. On the other hand, your son's brain will cooperate, think, and exert effort if (and only if) you are willing to intervene and commit to making sure he has the following four critical conditions in place: awareness, belief, support and skin in the reading game.

If any of these conditions aren't present or become unavailable too early in the process, your son's brain will give up on trying and go back to his familiar non-reading habit.

Below are the four conditions and what they mean for your son:

1) **Awareness:** Before any transformation can happen, the first thing you must do is make your son aware that his non-reading habit exists and why that concerns you. Because you are now aware why the reading habit is so important, you can confidently share your concerns with your son.
2) **Belief:** Once your son is fully aware of the situation, it's up

to him to decide if he believes the benefits of the reading habit are worth his time, effort and investment for his future success and, if so, then he must believe that he can change. This is why you must come to the table believing in your son and in the importance of the reading habit before you can expect him to believe in it himself.

3) **Support:** Your son must have a community—even if it's just a community of one—in his corner to help him maintain his belief that he can do it, especially when the going gets tough (because it will). By committing to being in the driver's seat, investing in your own reading life, and learning how to balance and adjust your son's reading habit, you are giving your son the gift of support that will make all the difference in the world.

4) **Skin in the reading game:** Your son must make a commitment and invest in his own reading habit; he must consciously accept the hard work, recognize that derailments will happen and—most importantly—know that he has control and a plan in place to make it happen and enable him to stay the course. By investing in your own reading habit and becoming the role model of walking and talking, you now have the empathy and stories your son will need to put skin in *his* reading game. When he sees that *you* can do it, he knows it's valuable and worth doing, and he can follow your example.

As you can probably understand by now, every building block prior to this one created the foundation for your son's reading habit to have the most viable chance of taking hold. Without Building Blocks 1–8 in place, it's like when a parent who smokes is trying to break the smoking habit in their teenager, or when an overweight parent who never exercises is trying to get their kid to eat healthy and run around outside.

When you—as the parent—aren't aware and don't believe, commit to support, invest, and have skin in the game, change and transformation in your son just isn't possible.

Because you pinpoint... you'll understand your son's non-reading habit loop.

For a habit to form, three elements—the cue, routine and reward—must be in place and working in concert to create what is known as the habit loop. Each of your son's habits brings its own habit loop to the table, and your son's non-reading habit is no different.

Right now your son has a cue (a person, place, time, object, smell, etc.) that triggers his non-reading habit loop. When he's exposed to this cue, his brain goes into automatic mode and starts craving the reward it expects to get, which then sets the action into motion. This action (physical/mental/or emotional) is your son's non-reading habit routine, but his brain is most excited about the intrinsic or extrinsic reward (pleasure/benefit/gain/outcome) it gets when your son exercises this routine.

The reward aspect is huge, because it's what his brain used to determine if the loop was worth remembering for the future, and now the craving for it drives your son to repeat his non-reading habit loop again.

Why does this matter?

Because for your son to successfully transform his non-reading habit into the reading habit, he must keep the same cue and reward he has now and just change his routine. In other words, whatever triggers the *non-reading* habit loop when your son comes home from school, after he does his homework or after dinner, must be the *exact same cue* he uses to trigger his new *reading* habit loop. In addition, his new reading habit must provide the same reward that he gets from not reading.

This means you must pinpoint your son's non-reading habit loop and then analyze it to determine the cue that triggers his brain and the reward it craves.

If you ever wondered why breaking habits feels impossible, now you know. When transforming an existing version of a habit (not reading, not exercising, smoking, eating unhealthy) into another version of the same habit (reading, exercising, not smoking, eating healthy), the only way it's possible is by keeping the same cue and reward and then to change the old routine by deliberately replacing it with the new one.

Think back to all the times you tried to get your son to read books in his spare time without this critical piece of information. How did it work out?

For me, it went terribly. At one point in my career, I believed that self-proclaiming non-reading boys should view reading itself as its own reward, end of story. I gave them time to read, access to books, and choice. I only thought of rewards in a unidimensional way: external and "bad." Without me realizing it, my belief consistently and unintentionally added pain to the boys' pleasure reading.

The Pizza Hut's Book It! reading program that was being carried out in the school was the opposite of my personal view about rewards. It was meant to get kids eager to read by giving them a coupon for an individual pizza, once a month, if they had completed the amount of reading that their teacher had assigned. Many teachers used it to get kids to do pleasure reading for homework. To check and make sure they had done the assigned reading, quizzes and summaries were part of the deal to get the coupon, which turned pleasure reading into mandatory reading.

Because I wanted boys to want to read for pleasure, I dug deep and researched how they responded to an adult-suggested, one-size-fits-all reward for reading, compared to no reward at all. It turned out that both led to the same result (boys not wanting to read for pleasure), but for different reasons.

My "no rewards" way *did* have boys reading books of their choice every day for 30 minutes, just not happily and very begrudgingly.

Here's a compilation of what boys who participated in Book It! shared about why it didn't transform their non-reading habit:

1) They hated pizza or Pizza Hut. Because they didn't crave the reward, they didn't pleasure read for homework. For many, not filling in their book chart or doing the required assignments affected their reading grade, but they didn't care and still wouldn't do it, because they wanted nothing to do with pizza.
2) They loved Pizza Hut and craved the reward, but hated reading, so they figured out ways around the reading. For many, a parent signed the form even though they hadn't read; some boys even signed for their parents. If they also had to write a summary or take a quiz, they'd skim, cheat, copy off of someone else (usually a girl), or try to "game" the system so they could get their pizza.

Most adults think *all* boys want food, money, video games and external rewards to get them to do things but, in reality, only a small number of boys crave those things.

To figure out what most boys craved instead, I researched, tinkered, observed and asked boys straight out what they liked most about the activities they did in their spare time. Below are the three rewards I pinpointed and included in everything I did, especially when it came to boys and reading for pleasure:

• Choice and freedom to decide what they wanted to do
• Being able to move around/not feel trapped
• Hanging out with their friends

Because you pinpoint... you'll know how to use your son's cues and rewards to transform his non-reading habit into the reading habit.

Each boy is different, but in my experience, I found that most boys crave one, two, or all three of these powerful rewards (choice, movement and social interaction). I share them as a starting place, so you can better understand where your son may be coming from in terms of his non-reading habit loop.

To help you go deeper with pinpointing cues and rewards, I created two different scenarios of self-proclaiming non-reading preteen/early teen boys who both have a non-reading habit loop, but for different reasons. From Building Block 8: Adjust, you'll also notice how the developmental differences between preteen boys and early teen boys play out in the scenarios; they are subtle, but critical.

Mom A: Her son is 10 years old. He loves watching TV, and can (and will) watch from the minute he comes home from school until dinner. When he was younger, that was their time together, but recently he needs more space and goes to the den to "be alone." Mom A recently realized her son now watches over three hours of TV every day, and it's all sitcoms. When she asked him why he watches sitcoms, he cracked up and told her that, after being told all day in school he needs to be "good and quiet," he loves how they make him laugh out loud. Mom A wants to balance her son's TV time with 30 minutes of pleasure reading, and after observing him for a few days, she thinks she has a great idea about how to do it.

Non-reading Activity: Watching television after school

Cue(s): Runs in the house from the bus, drops his backpack in the hallway, heads straight to the pantry and grabs a bag of chips.

Routine: He plops on the couch, puts his feet up, turns on the television in the den where no one can bother him, eats chips and watches his favorite sitcoms until dinner.

Reward(s): entertainment, laughing, choice, freedom from dealing with adults, comfort

(Don't worry about the reading routine right now; you will be going deeper with it in Building Block 10: Planning.)

See the chart on the next page, which shows how these elements relate to each other.

Routine: New	Cue(s): Same	Reward(s): Same	New Habit Loop: Exchange Watching TV with Reading
Reading for 30 minutes right after school	Drop backpack in hallway, grab bag of chips from pantry	Entertainment, laughing, choice, freedom from dealing with adults, comfort	**Cue**: Time—right after he runs into the house. Continue to drop his bag in the hallway and grab the chips from the pantry. **Routine**: Instead of den, he goes to the basement. Instead of couch, he plops in his fort. Instead of turning on the TV, he chooses a joke book to read. Instead of watching sitcoms, he reads joke books. Continues to eat chips. **Reward(s):** Entertainment/laughing: joke books Choice: of reading material and spot Freedom from adults/comfort: in basement/in fort

Why this might work: Mom A exchanges the routine of watching a 30-minute sitcom with reading humorous books of his choice for 30 minutes instead.

Mom B: Her son is 13 years old and lately has become attached to texting on his cell phone and a new group of friends who play soccer after school. She knows her son would rather watch paint dry than play soccer, so it surprises her how much he begs her to let him go play. Now that he's a teenager, so many things are changing with him, she decided to ask him instead of assume. When she did, he said he still can't stand soccer, but he's itchy from being in school all day, just sitting, and he's got to get out. When she told him he could go outside without waiting for a text, he rolled his eyes, and said disparagingly, "Tsk! Mom, really!"

Now instead of doing his homework, he sits at the dining room table and stares at his phone. When he doesn't get a text by 4:30 p.m., he doodles on his homework, notebooks, and his hand until dinner. Because he's distracted, his homework isn't getting done. Mom B wants her son to start balancing his schedule with 30 minutes of reading, and after observing him for a few days, she thinks she has a great idea how to do it.

Non-reading Activity: Soccer with friends in the park down the street or sitting at the table doodling instead of doing his homework

Cue: His friend sends a text to his cell phone around 4:30 p.m., during homework time at the dining room table (not every day, but he waits for it each day).

Routine: He jumps up from the table, runs into the kitchen, begs, says he'll be home by 6 p.m. for dinner and will finish his homework after dinner, after which he runs out the door.

Reward(s): social interaction with peers, being invited, being outdoors, movement

Routine: New	Cue: Same	Reward(s): Same	New Habit Loop: Exchange Soccer with Reading
Reading for 30-minutes outside with friend(s)	A text invitation from a friend on his cell phone	Social interaction with peers, being invited, being outdoors, movement	**Cue**: A text invitation from a friend on his cell phone **Routine**: Instead of waiting and hoping for an invitation, the text will be planned ahead of time. Instead of not finishing his homework, he'll work on his homework because he will know the plan. Instead of playing soccer, a group of boys will read outside for 30 minutes and then run around at the park until 6 p.m. **Reward:** The rewards are all the same

Why this might work: Mom B knows her son doesn't really like to play soccer or care for the new friends; it's more about getting the text on his phone and running around outside with other people after being kept sitting in school all day He has a few friends who read, so she'll create a plan to include them.

Both Mom A and Mom B observed their sons to determine the best time to balance distractors with 30 minutes of pleasure reading, and then they pinpointed the cues and rewards for the non-reading routine. In addition to their observations, they used what they knew about their sons, but realizing that their sons are changing, they made sure to ask questions and find out how they were currently thinking.

ACTION STEPS

1. Tough Question: Do you know what your son's non-reading habit looks like—what triggers it (cue), his routine while doing it, and the reward(s) he craves from it—so you can transform it into the reading habit?

Probably not, and you're not alone. This is the missing link on how to finally transform your preteen/early teen son's not-so-great habits. Even though it requires intentional, up-front planning on your part, think how much nicer it will be to work with your son when you know what he craves and what his brain wants. Habits create neurological cravings, and your son craves his reward before it comes. His cravings are what drive his habits. Pinpointing his *non-reading habit* cue and its associated reward is key to transforming it into the 30-minute-a-day *reading habit.*

2. Pinpoint your son's non-reading cues and rewards: The good news is that you're not starting with a blank slate and no information. You have *lots* of information that you can use to create some hypotheses about your son's possible cues and rewards: your background knowledge, his developmental needs (from the chart in Building Block 8: Adjust), your observations from the action steps you took in Building Blocks 5 and 7, and the rewards I incorporated every day so boys actually enjoyed reading for pleasure (choice, movement, and social interaction).

OLBE will help you to think and plan ahead.

Observe: This time, "observing" means to re-read your observations about your son as he currently is and other key information about how most preteen/early teen boys operate at this stage in their lives. Re-read your notes through the lens of cues and rewards.

What are some things that you notice may trigger your son's non-reading habit, and what are some possible rewards he might crave from this activity? Also re-read the developmental needs chart, to see if there might be anything you may have missed during your first reading. Remember, different activities (routines) have different cues and rewards. Pay attention to them *all* right now, because the more you know, the more confident and less frustrated you'll feel when you try to meet your son where he stands today.

List: In a notebook or the workbook, generate a list of all of your son's non-reading activities, the cues you think trigger each activity, and the rewards you think your son craves from the activity. Use the scenarios I shared earlier to guide you, but remember, don't worry about the routine of the activity, just name the activity for now.

Brainstorm: Using the list above and the one you generated in Building Block 7: Balance (five times in your son's day where pleasure reading might work and for how long), think through which times make the most sense to build a plan around. Pay attention to the cues that trigger the activities and the pay-off in terms of their rewards for your son.

Another way to think about rewards is to capitalize on the benefits of reading. Maybe there are times when adding reading as the reward will actually do your son a world of good in other ways, too.

For example, if he takes too long doing homework every night because he's distracted, by incorporating 10–30 minutes of pleasure reading, he'll relax, become less stressed and more focused. A pleasure reading break may be just what he needs to finish his homework. Or maybe your son plays video games before he goes to bed every night. Unlike pleasure reading (which is relaxing), research has found that video games *add* to already existing stress, instead of helping to eliminate it. Imagine the return on investment if your son exchanged a book for a video game to end each day. Not only will he get smarter, but his sleep will improve, too.

Brainstorm those times that may give your son a greater return on his investment than other times. Do any of these times overlap the other times that may work? Write those times down and include the activity, cue and reward.

Explore: Over the next couple of days, explore what you have been hypothesizing about your son's activities, cues and rewards. Watch to see if your son has changed at all since you last observed him, if you missed something earlier you want to add, and to double check before you pinpoint. If you have questions, ask your son by using the strategy I shared in Building Block 4: Walk the Talk. Remember, he probably won't be able to express a clear, articulate reason, but you'll definitely get the gist of it. Now that you are aware of and understand your son's BAG needs, and you recognize that his brain likes things to be easy, you'll have a better sense of how to frame your conversation, when to push, and when to move on.

After you explore, it's time to pinpoint at least two possible pleasure-reading times (with their cues and rewards) where, instead of seeing reading as a cost or pain, your son will see it as a benefit worth his time, effort and investment for future success. In Building Block 10: Plan, you will use these times, cues and rewards to draft flexible routines to share with your son.

KEY TAKEAWAYS... Building Block 9: Pinpoint

- Your son's non-reading habit formed unintentionally, but because the brain and habits are malleable, he can turn this around. Through intentional design, his *non-reading* habit can be transformed into his *reading* habit.
- Without your willingness to commit and intervene, your son won't be able to create the four critical conditions that he needs to be in place in order to change his non-reading habit: awareness, belief, support and skin in the reading game.
- Knowing your son's non-reading habit loop (cue, routine and reward) is the key to its transformation.
- An established unintentional habit can be transformed to its more beneficial version (non-reading habit to the reading habit), but only if the cue and reward stay the same. The routine is the only part of the loop that changes.

Once you pinpoint two possible pleasure-reading times (with their cues and rewards), it's time to dive into Building Block 10: Plan and begin the work to create new reading habit routines.

Visit the link below to download the "Trigger Checklist" I created for you.

This checklist will help you determine your son's triggers (cues) that prompt him to start craving his non-reading activity reward(s).

www.hillarytubin.com/freetriggerchecklist

❧ BUILDING BLOCK 10: PLAN ❧

Your son needs you to plan ahead before instilling
the 30-minute-a-day reading habit in him.

THE RIPPLE EFFECTS OF PLANNING

**Because you plan... you will recognize the 5 default
initiator personalities.**

There was a time in my career when I didn't plan ahead or think
about what boys needed from me to become a reader. I truly
believed that, if I provided the time and gave them access to and
choice in what books they wanted to read and where they wanted
to sit, they'd be so happy and appreciative, they'd just do it.

Yeah, well not so much. Here's what 15 minutes of pleasure reading
looked like instead:

*Girls cozying up with a book in their spot, happily reading. Boys
roaming around the classroom, scanning the bookshelves for a
book to read. This was something I expected they did on their
own, ahead of time, but boys always waited until reading time
to find a book. Eventually, I'd become frustrated and send them
back to their seats (not their cozy reading spots), with books I
pulled off the shelf at random for them to read. Back in their seats,
they reluctantly opened the books, but mostly they stared at the
clock, their hands, their shoes, their friends' shoes, or the ceiling.
When I would see them not reading, I'd go into high gear and yap
at them about the importance of reading during reading time
and how they were missing out. They'd give me a blank stare
until I was done yapping and reading time was over.*

So many things are wrong with this picture, I'm sure that after reading Building Blocks 1–8 you're shaking your head right now. Me, too.

I call this phase my Referee/Commentator/Spectator period.

Let me explain.

I didn't have my epiphany until the boys from the above snapshot started inviting me to their weekend soccer and basketball games. Week after week, I watched those boys come to life on the field and court. At every game I attended, those same boys who had searched aimlessly for a book during reading time were prepared and ready to play the game as soon as they showed up. When asked why that was so, they could articulate for me exactly what their coaches expected and why. If someone asked them those same questions during reading time, they'd say, "Huh? What?"

What mesmerized me the most was watching the boys interact with their coaches on and off the field and court. The same boys who had stared at me blankly met their coach's instructions, demands, and feedback with rapt attention, respect and responsiveness. It was clear they were all working together towards a common goal, and they all had skin in the game. I wanted that, too—for reading!

To figure out what was going on, I questioned their coaches on why they thought this might be happening and how I might fix it.

What they shared, and what the boys confirmed, messed with my head at first, but then it made all the sense in the world.

In a nutshell, what they said was this: "Good coaches know boys need routines, structures, and practice if they want them to succeed. Boys just don't do well when things are all loosey-goosey. That's when they fall apart. Boys need to know exactly what is expected of them, down to the smallest detail: show them, correct them, have them practice, give them specific feedback. And then, if they don't follow through, call them out on it by explaining why you believe in them and expect them to step up to the game. If you don't, they stop believing that you mean what you say and say what you mean."

Ouch. Not being male or having had anyone explain to me what boys needed to succeed, I had definitely missed the mark on how to help them cultivate a habit.

I really thought I had created the perfect reading environment for boys by using what I knew at the time. I provided time to read in school, cool spots to read in, access to a ton of books, and the freedom to choose their spots and books without any interference from me. I knew choice and movement mattered, so I used those rewards to entice boys into reading as fun. However, when the enticing didn't work the magic I believed it would, we ended up going round and round in a reactive rut: I called foul and yapped at them, they stared at me, and the next day it happened all over again.

That's why I call this my Referee/Commentator/Spectator period. I was anything *but* a coach!

Continuing with the sports analogy, here's how I now understand what boys need from adults to successfully instill the 30-minute-a-day-reading habit in them.

Think of a football game. There are six different roles people play, each with a specific personality, to support the players on the team—coach, cheerleader, referee, commentator, mascot and spectator—but only one of those roles (the coach) is directly responsible for being the primary source of substantial support/expectations/strategy/and feedback for both the individual players and the team as a whole to ensure success. The other roles are what I call "superficial support." They only show up on game day, and their roles and personalities only interact with the individual players indirectly.

Below are what I call *The 6 Initiator Personalities* adults take on when trying to instill the reading habit in preteen/early teen boys. Like it had been with me, when no planning and practice ahead of time takes place, you may even end up with multiple-initiator personality disorder. When you read the personality descriptors of each role, you'll start to become aware of your own initiator personality, which is the first step of understanding why being a coach is the way to go.

The 6 Initiator Personalities

Substantial Support

The Coach: plans ahead, strategizes, adjusts and provides routines, structures, expectations, practice and specific feedback that will ensure reading success for boys.

Superficial Support

The Cheerleader: motivates boys from a distance with enthusiasm, jumping up and down, and cheering them on, saying things like, "You can do it!" so they'll want to read.

The Referee: enforces certain reading rules and calls "Foul!" for non-compliance when boys don't follow the rules (even if they were never explained and/or practiced).

The Commentator: comments critically about what's happening and publicly expresses their opinions about boys and their reading, but doesn't help them make changes.

The Mascot: distracts boys away from reading by allowing them to engage in activities that provide fun and relief from doing something that they don't enjoy.

The Spectator: pays a currency (money/time/opportunity) to watch boys read (from a distance, with no involvement) and because a currency was paid, still expects reading success to happen.

It's easy to see why boys respond best to the coach personality. It gives them everything they secretly need to become a reader, but don't know how to ask for. The other personalities act in ways that don't meet the boys' needs, which leads them to continue to avoid reading.

Because you plan... you will become your son's coach.

In the snapshot I gave of how I used to try to motivate boys to read, imagine what that would have looked like if I had taken the time to put routines, structures and expectations in place for the boys, prior to reading time. A very different picture indeed!

Instead of sitting back like a spectator, doing nothing but expecting success from afar, I should have planned ahead, shared my expectations, provided access to the books prior to reading time, coached them on the art of choosing a pleasure-reading book, and then watched as they practiced so I could provide specific feedback to help them become better at what they were doing. Because I didn't do those things, the boys weren't prepared for reading time and never had a chance to read, while I quickly spiraled from spectator to referee to commentator.

No one walked away a winner, least of all the boys.

After talking to the boys' coaches, I decided to study Vince Lombardi and learn what made him tick. He is considered one of the best and most successful football coaches in NFL history, and even though he died in 1970, his legacy on what it takes to succeed lives on in his many thought-provoking, inspirational quotes. Below I share three of my favorites and how they influenced my boy-responsive reading mindset and environment.[67]

1. *"Once you have established the goals you want and the price you're willing to pay, you can ignore the minor hurts, the opponent's pressure and the temporary failures."*

By planning ahead and visualizing boys reading, increasing their vocabulary, strengthening their cognitive skills, and becoming more interesting people, I knew that —come heck or high-water— boys in my class would read for pleasure. As their coach, I also knew this meant I had to wear my metaphorical Teflon skin to school when I instilled the reading habit because it wasn't always pretty: teeth-sucking "tsks," eye rolling, excuses, stonewalling, more excuses, notes from parents—you name it. But I stayed the course every day because, to me, the goal was worth it.

Your son isn't going to make instilling his reading habit smooth sailing for you, but if you truly think 30 minutes of pleasure reading every day is a worthy goal, then—as his coach—you'll be willing to pay the price.

2. *"There's only one way to succeed in anything, and that is to give it everything. I do, and I demand that my players do."*

Coaches know that it takes their investment *and* each individual player's investment to succeed. The same needs to apply when coaching your son on the reading habit. You need to mean business. You must stand firm with your belief that he will read for pleasure, and you must invest skin in the game so he will do the same.

3. *"It is essential to understand that battles are primarily won in the hearts of men. Men respond to leadership in a most remarkable way and once you have won his heart, he will follow you anywhere."*

Once I fully understood a boy's heart and wasn't afraid to make a stand for the goal of pleasure reading, everything shifted. Your son is waiting for you to lead him to read, to get into the driver's seat. Because it's not until you confidently use your knowledge of reading's benefits and distractors, your awareness of how to appreciate a variety of boy-friendly reading material and forms, and your understanding of the demands on his time and his developmental needs, that you'll win his heart and he will follow.

Because you plan... you will have in place the 4 Ws to ensure your son has access to books and can find ones he likes to read.

When I asked boys why they didn't read, the number 1 response was usually not being able to find books they liked to read.

Scholastic's report confirms my finding. When boys were asked whether they agreed with the statement, "I would read more if I could find more books that I like," 76% of boys ages 9–11 agreed and 79% of boys ages 12–14 agreed.

For many boys, this is where their reading habit breaks down. If they can't find something they like to read, then they won't read.

Before I realized this, I was part of the problem. Even though I provided access to a ton of reading material I knew boys would love, they still wandered aimlessly in front of shelves, just staring, not knowing what to do. Instead of helping them, I behaved like a spectator, and expected them to pick out books themselves without any direction from me and they became frustrated when they couldn't find one that they liked.

I wasn't alone. Over the years, when boys couldn't find a book to read, I found many teachers and parents fell into one of the following initiator personalities: spectator, cheerleader, commentator, mascot or referee.

- The spectator expects boys to be able to pick out their own books without help.
- The cheerleader enthusiastically tells boys they can do it, they'll find a book, keep looking.
- The commentator critically comments on any books boys choose that are "low brow" or they find "inappropriate."
- The mascot distracts boys by showing movies and letting them play games on the computer instead.
- The referee punishes boys for not finding a book.

It's the coach who plans ahead and strategizes, so that boys are successful at finding books to read.

Below are four questions to help you think like a coach.

- **Who** will work with your son to make sure he has reading material he likes?
- **Where** will your son find and access reading material?
- **When** will he browse and choose his reading material?
- **What** routines and structures will be in place to make sure reading material is ready, prior to his reading time?

Who

Coaches are the primary support, but they know they can't do it alone. Many have assistant coaches and parents help them carry the load. If not, the load can get awfully heavy.

When I became a coach, I enlisted librarians, teachers, parents and other adults—grandparents, babysitters, aunts, uncles, student teachers, tutors, and volunteers—to step up and assist me with helping boys find books they wanted to read, prior to reading time. I also created "Reading Office Hours" for one hour before school started. Boys were able to come to school early, browse the books and get help from me, and in the afternoons both the school and public librarians were available for support.

All on your own, you can't help your son find the books he likes to read. It's important for you to think of the people and resources that are available and might be able to help.

Here's an example of what your list might look like:

- You: you can help him look online for books and reading material to print and read.
- His dad: he's been wanting to share this bizarre graphic novel

with your son (some book he loved as a kid) and get him into comic books.

- His teacher: she has a lot of books in her classroom and has offered help in the past, but maybe you never got around to doing anything about her offer.
- His grandmother: she lives close by and goes to the library every Friday afternoon; she'd love to take him with her and then they could go grab a snack together afterwards.
- The public librarian: when he was in third grade, she used to help him find books he always loved; she's still there and you're sure she would be happy to help.

When I was a kid, the public librarian in my neighborhood always had a pile of books for me to take out and read each week. For years, she was the person who kept books in my hands.

Librarians come to work every day to help people connect with books. Don't overlook your library and the people who are there, waiting and wanting to help your son connect with books.

Where

Research shows that easy access to books can make all the difference as to whether boys read or not. Unfortunately, for some boys, access is determined because of where they live. They may not have a public library nearby due to budget cuts/constraints and/or their school is under-resourced and the school library is closed.

For other boys, they do have easy access to a public library, school library, and plenty of books to read in their classrooms and homes, but because reading isn't valued, they're mentally disconnected from their access to books. It's meaningless to them, and therefore they do not appreciate or utilize it.

Parents are instrumental in both of these situations. When you care about books and realize their value in your son's life, you'll connect the dots for him so that he not only has *access* to books, he'll understand and appreciate what access to books means and represents for his future success. He needs *you* to make him aware of his surroundings and what's available.

There are so many ways and places to secure reading material for boys and connect them with books. It's actually amazing. Some cost money. Some are free. But once you start thinking about where your son can find reading material, the possibilities are endless.

Below is a list to get you thinking:

Scholastic Book Fair
Scholastic Book Order
Classroom Libraries
School Library
Receive books as gifts
Flea Markets and Garage Sales
Internet: Amazon/Kindle Store, Barnes and Noble, Project Gutenberg
Store: Barnes and Noble, Comic Book Store, Target/Walmart
Public Library
Audible.com
Newspapers/Magazines (delivered to house, purchase at store)
Your home/or people you know
Book swap with friends/relatives/neighbors/classmates

You know your community, your particular circumstances, and your son's age/level of independence, so different options will work better than others at various times. It's important to also think about whether your son requires assistance and what kind of assistance he might need (driving, purchasing (money/credit card/check) or a password).

The more you can think through your son's access to books and make it easy for him, the more likely it will be that he reads.

When

The next big W is all about scheduling time for your son to choose his books. Remember that this specific time is separate from the two possible reading times you came up with in Building Block 9: Pinpoint.

Because scheduling can be a nightmare, figuring out the *when* will come after you know *who* can support you and *where* your son can access reading material. Using the list of possible support that I shared in the Who section, I'll show you an example of how to plan ahead and think through When.

Imagine your son's dad likes comics and is willing to take him to the comic book store once a month. You check your son's schedule, and it seems like the last Saturday of every month works the best. Since his grandmother goes to the library every Friday afternoon, maybe she can pick up your son from school on the way to the library. You know your son respects his teacher, and she said at parent/teacher conferences that her library is open, and she's available to help. Your son doesn't have any activities on Monday, so maybe it's time to check with the teacher and see if he can stay after school, and they can work together to find him books. You may realize Sundays are a great day for you and your son to browse the Kindle Store and talk about books he may want to read.

3 Ws Chart			
Who	**Where**	**When**	**Assistance**
Dad	Comic Book Store	Last Saturday of the month	Drive, purchase
Grandmother/ Librarian	Public Library	Fridays after school	Drive
Literacy Teacher	Classroom Library	Monday after school	
You	Kindle Store	Sundays	Purchase, password
Son	School Library	Tuesday with his class	

Every time I worked with parents and boys whose schedules were packed, planning ahead and thinking through the 3 Ws chart usually opened up a ton of possibilities. If this was your brainstorm chart, and you had checked in with everyone and they had all agreed to help, imagine sitting with your son and letting him figure out his book-choosing schedule. Like a coach, you did the legwork, the planning ahead that was necessary to connect the dots for him, and now, instead of wandering aimlessly, your son will have support and succeed because of it.

What

For your son to transform his non-reading habit to the reading habit, he needs consistency, structure and routines. Everything related to the reading habit should become automatic, like a well-oiled machine, and something he can depend on.

Before I became a coach, I hated consistency, structure and routines; I thought they were stifling to creativity, freedom, choice and autonomy. So I operated in a very "loosey-goosey" way, expecting that this lack of structure would naturally bring out an innate joy in learning, the spirit of intellectual curiosity, and creative genius in all of my students. Mmm, not so much.

Once I got over myself and implemented what my boys needed, everything changed.

The new structure I created for reading time was consistent each day for 15 minutes, and it was non-negotiable to show up at reading time without a book. Ahead of time, we sat down together, and I explained the structure and the routines in a clear, direct way. I told them when they could count on reading time and what that time would look like, sound like and feel like. Then I broke down for them *where* they could find books, *when* they could find books, *who* would be there to help them find books, and *how* they could find books. I also included what would happen if they derailed and how they could count on me to help them get back on track as quick as possible.

They asked questions. I had them rehearse and practice by doing it ahead of time. I provided specific feedback and helped correct any issues upfront. After practicing, the boys had a chance to share what worked and what didn't, and when appropriate, modifications and changes were made to the structure and routines.

With this group of boys, not only did reading time dramatically change, but every year after that, by starting as a coach and making my structures, routines and expectations as clear and easy to follow as possible, I achieved the same successful results time and again: the boys read.

The 3 Ws Chart is a great place to start thinking about routines your son might need to find books. Using the above chart as an example, I created a list of possible routines that need to be established and rehearsed in order for success to occur.

- Because he normally walks, how to meet his grandmother in her car after school on Friday's routine: how to wait until the car pick-ups are called at the end of the day, how to stand with the safety guard until his grandmother's car is next in line.
- What it will look like for the finding a book in the library routine: how to approach the librarian who is there to help him, how to decide what books to take out, what to do with the books he doesn't want to take out, what to do while he waits for his grandmother to be finished.
- What it will look like to in the meet his literacy teacher after school routine: where he should go after dismissed from homeroom, how he should wait for his teacher, what he should do after he finds a book and is ready to leave

Boys pretend that they don't need routines laid out for them, but they do. As the literacy teacher the boys were coming to see, here's the biggest reason the boys shared with me as to why they didn't show up at my room and went home instead.

They heard, "Don't forget you're meeting your teacher after school today," but they had a lot of unanswered questions about what it really meant. For example: do they go to her room and wait outside the door; do they just go in and sit in their literacy seats; do they just head to the classroom library and start looking; will the teacher talk to them or sit at her desk; what do they do when they're done looking, etc.?

All these unanswered questions confused the boys and created anxiety, and it was easier and more comfortable for them to walk out the front door like they always did. Then, when questioned, because the instructions given to them were unclear, they had a ready list of excuses to explain why they didn't go to the teacher's room after school.

Simple routines, with no more than three steps, work best for boys to remember. I found that their brains preferred to hear, "Do this. Do this. Do this." Just like *too few* words are problematic, *too many* words are, too. If routines and directions become long-winded and wordy, boys actually get stuck on the extra words, and that's what they will follow instead.

Here's an example of setting the purpose and expectation up front, followed by a clear, easy-to-follow three-step routine:

For the next four Mondays, your teacher will expect you after school so she can help you find books to read.

1) When you're dismissed from homeroom, she said to wait outside her room, next to the window.
2) When she's ready, she'll come to the door and invite you in.
3) When you're done, walk directly home and put the new books next to your reading spot.

Yes, your son will suck on his teeth, glare at you, and think you don't trust him. Teflon skin. Say it anyway, and then have him repeat what he needs to do out loud, so you can verify that he has heard what you said. Some of my boys' parents even had their sons write routines on a post-it note and put it in their assignment book each Monday. Anything so they would have a book to read.

ACTION STEPS

1. Tough Question: In the past, did you plan ahead for the success of your son's reading habit?

Most parents don't think of getting their son to read as something they need to plan ahead. By the time he's a preteen/early teen there are so many other things going on, and in their thinking, he should be old enough to do it on his own. He can't. In addition, most adults provide only superficial support when it comes to boys and their reading habit, rather than the substantial support they desperately need. Boys need a reading habit coach. Your son needs *you* to be a reading habit coach for him.

2. Know your default initiation personality: Once you're aware of how your personality shifts when you help your son with reading and have no plan in place, you're ready to make the leap to be his substantial support—his coach.

Superficial Support

The Cheerleader: Do you motivate your son to read by enthusiastically cheering things like, "Reading's good for you! You've got this! You're smart!" when he says he hates reading?

The Referee: Do you find yourself being the reading enforcer, bad guy and foul-giver when your son doesn't read the way you expect him to read?

The Commentator: Are you unable to stop yourself from making critical comments and expressing your opinion to your son and others about how and what your son reads?

The Mascot: Because you know your son doesn't like to read, do you allow him to engage in fun reading-distractor activities he enjoys instead?

The Spectator: As a taxpayer and/or busy working parent, do you watch your son's reading from a distance, with no involvement but with high expectations, because you believe it's the school's responsibility to get your son to read?

- Take a moment to remember a time when you tried to get your son to read without a plan? Were you confident going into it? Was the interaction with your son harmonious? Would you say the outcome was a success? Or if you never tried to get your son to read, think about a time when he wasn't reading and why you didn't approach him.
- With the moment in mind, read through the initiation personalities listed above and choose which one best reflects you. Maybe you became more than one personality like I did. Jot down your initiation personality(s) in your notebook or workbook.
- To shift from superficial support to substantial support, it's important to first become aware of what your superficial support looks like, sounds like and feels like. If not, it's very easy to fall back into what you've always done. Once you're aware, you can catch yourself before it's too late and shift back into being a coach.
- In your notebook or workbook, jot down your answers to the following questions about the initiation moment. Try to capture as much as you can. Use my snapshot as an example.

  If you're a mascot or spectator, think about what was happening when you chose not to approach your son about his reading.

  - What were the words and tone you used to initiate your son's reading?
  - What was your body language? Were you standing and waving your arms? Smiling or frowning?
  - What did you do after he responded to your suggestion?
  - What did you feel during and afterwards?
- Now take a moment and embrace your initiation personality and everything about it. You were doing your very best for your

son at the time, and this personality you relied on came out because you weren't sure what else to do. Now you are aware and knowledgeable, and you realize that your son needed something very specific from you to be successful with his reading habit.

3. Planning ahead for the 4 Ws: For preteen/early teen boys, finding time to read is not their biggest barrier to reading, it's finding books they like and want to read. The coach is the only initiation personality able to take this huge "make or break" non-reading reason into account and strategize for its success.

OLBE will help you to think and plan ahead like a coach.

Observe: Start to pay attention to the people around you who are available to support you and help your son find books he likes. Keep an open mind about this, and it's amazing to see the people who will present themselves to you. While you think about *who*, also think about *where* your son can access books and *when* he can access them prior to his reading time.

List: Fill in the 3 Ws chart below. Contact the people in the Who column to enlist their support and jot down their responses. Make any changes based on their responses.

Who	Where	When	Assistance	Contacted and Response

Brainstorm: Looking at the chart, brainstorm the routines you might need to establish so that your son knows what he needs to do to find books. Make a list of as many routines the 3 Ws chart brings to mind.

Explore: Try your hand at writing out the what, expectations and three-step routines, using ideas from your brainstorm list. This requires thinking ahead and, if necessary, checking in with the other supporters on your list. It's not always easy to pare down what you're saying to the barest, most explicit essentials, but for boys to wrap their heads around what's expected and how it's expected, you need to speak to them in the language they hear best.

4. Think like a coach and create your playbook before instilling the reading habit in your son: Coaches know the value of having a playbook (a notebook containing a compilation of descriptions, instructions, strategies and diagrams). After they assess the situation at hand (their players, the opponents, etc.), they utilize this information to plan their game-day approach. Having what they need at their fingertips is how coaches develop thoughtful and mindful game plans for their players to practice and execute.

Without a playbook, success isn't a possibility.

"The price of success is hard work, dedication to the job at hand, and the determination that whether we win or lose, we have applied the best of ourselves to the task at hand."—Vince Lombardi

Creating the Reading Habit Playbook

The Action Step notes you need to have available are the following:

Building Block 1, Believe, Action Step #2: Letter to your son

Building Block 2, Invest, Action Step #2: Your reading story

Building Block 3, Read, Action Step #3: List of male reading role models ready to support your son's reading habit

Building Block 4, Walk and Talk, Action Step #3: Your rehearsal notes on how to talk to your son

Building Block 5, Prioritize, Action Step # 3: Your re-allocated schedule that includes reading in your family's life

Building Block 6, Appreciate, Action Steps #2 and #3: The list of possible books your son might want to read and spots he might want to read in

Building Block 7, Balance, Action Step # 2: Your notes on your son's reading distractors, time spent on them and hot button distractors

Building Block 8, Adjust, Actions Step #2 and #3: The best time of year to ignite your son's reading habit and his current BAG needs

Building Block 9, Pinpoint, Action Step #2: Your son's non-reading habit cues and rewards

Building Block 10, Plan, Action Step #3: Your notes from planning the 4 Ws ahead of time so your son finds books to read

Visit the following link to download the playbook template I created for you.

Using your notes, fill in the template and follow the directions for the next steps found on the template.

www.hillarytubin.com/freeplaybooktemplate.

KEY TAKEAWAYS... Building Block 10: Plan

- Everyone has an initiation personality (coach, cheerleader, commentator, mascot, referee or spectator) that emerges when trying to get a preteen/early teen boy to read.
- Only the coach initiation personality will help boys succeed with their reading habit.
- It's imperative to not only plan a boy's reading time ahead of time, but also a separate time for him to find books he wants to read.
- Use the 4 Ws—who, where, when and what—to plan ahead for helping boys find books they want to read.

To show what's possible when you're boy-responsive, below are excerpts I received from boys who were once **self-proclaimed non-readers.** The purpose for sharing them is to inspire you, encourage you, and show you how your son can change.

"Over the three years of middle school, I learned how to become a dedicated student of literature. In these three years of hard work and commitment, I learned more than I could ever imagine. When I entered into the unknown world of high school, I felt prepared and well equipped to take on the challenges of ninth grade English. As I continue through high school, college, and beyond, I will always remember Ms. T and her literacy class, which has given me the tools to develop a deeper understanding of literature."—15-year-old boy reader

"I have many memories [about reading books] that either embar-rass me or make me look back with fondness. Embarrassment when I remember my obsession with fantasy books in sixth grade and resisting any other book. But my fond memories are from seventh and eighth grade, like reading Animal Farm, *and now I am really enjoying Shakespeare."*—14-year-old boy reader

"What you have done to shape my life is more than can be described in words. You have not only taught me literacy in a superb manner, you have helped me mature into who I am today. Coming into sixth grade, I felt like I owned the world, literacy wise. My earlier teachers said I was past college level as reading goes. But that was just being a "reader." I knew nothing about being a student of literature. But I simply did not have the "fire in my belly" to do anything about it. What you did was give me the cold, hard truth about what was happening and what was going to happen to me, and what you did seemed to work... Not only did you help shape who I am today and give a top-notch literacy education, you opened up the world to me... If I am my future self, and I look back at this moment, I would consider these three years the most memorable of my life."—14-year-old boy reader

"In the beginning of the year I didn't really like to read every night, because nobody made me do that before and I wasn't used to it. But somehow, someway you turned my whole life around. You helped me realize the importance of books and the impor-tance of the world."—11-year-old boy reader

Congratulations! You did it! You have now completed the work necessary to create the boy-responsive reading environment your son needs.

This means you:

1. Appreciate what your son will read.
2. Understand how to balance the 6 common reading distractors with 30 minutes of pleasure reading.
3. Know how to adjust your son's schedule for the seasons and also how to adjust your expectations by keeping his BAG needs in the forefront.
4. Discovered the cues and rewards of your son's non-reading habit.
5. Are set to be your son's reading habit coach and have planned and strategized in your reading habit playbook.

You are aware, knowledgeable and prepared! For one more burst of confidence before you instill the reading habit, read the Conclusion to see just how ready you are!

ఞ CONCLUSION: Ready to Initiate ఞ

"Give a man a fish and you feed him for a day. Teach a man to fish and you feed him for a lifetime."—Anne Isabella Thackeray Ritchie

Another way to look at being the coach your son needs during the three phases of his Reading Habit Journey (initiate, transform, nurture) is realizing that you're coaching him to develop a habit that will feed him for a lifetime. This means you will gradually release the responsibility to him. I suggest 90 days as a goal because this is how long it took most of my boys to become independent and have agency. Some took longer, depending on how badly they derailed, and that was okay. They just started their 90 days over again.

On the following page, I share with you two different first-person accounts of initiating, transforming and nurturing the reading habit with a preteen/early teen boy. They are both compiled from real stories of moms who wanted their preteen/early teen sons to read books.

Journey: teach to fish	Race: give a fish
Beginning: Every night for a few weeks, I read on the couch so my son could see me. Then before initiating, I set aside time to have an honest conversation with him about reading, why it matters, and how I want to bring more reading into both our lives. I shared the changes I made and why, and then together we figured out where he stands with his reading habit. Then we strategized and created a reading habit plan we both could live with that would take him from where he was to his ultimate goal: reading books of his choice on his own for 30 minutes every day. To aim for success, we made sure there were weekly check-in chats along the way, and time and speed stayed flexible because the main focus was his independence.	*Beginning*: One night all I wanted was some peace and quiet, except my son's video game was really annoying me. That's when I decided this was as good a time as any to initiate the reading habit like his teacher told me to do last month during parent/teacher conferences. So I told my son it's time he gets cracking with his reading. I let him know all the reasons he has to do it, and I explained to him how he's going to do it. I was really clear with him about the three-week time-frame it takes to build a habit, and that I expected him to read on his own at the end of 21 days. I told him that on day 22, I'll no longer be the one reminding him what he needs to do.
Middle: Because my son felt mornings were better for him, he set an alarm and got himself up to read every day. He kept track of his reading on a chart taped to the fridge and expected me to ask how it was going with his book each day. During the first weekly check-in chat, my son realized the initial goal we set was too challenging. Together we problem-solved solutions and decided to break the goal into smaller chunks. Each week during our check-in, he added more time to the smaller goal until he finally reached his destination.	*Middle*: Every night for 21 days I reminded him when it was time to read. I set a timer for him and told him not to get up until it binged, and then I would go to the kitchen and clean up, watch some television or check Facebook. Every few minutes I checked on him to make sure he was reading, and if he was I said, "Good job!" to keep him motivated. When the timer binged he jumped right up to go play his video games for the rest of the night. At least I had 30 minutes of peace.

Journey: teach to fish	Race: give a fish
End: It took my son 30 days to read the full 30 minutes. He started at 5 minutes and every 5 days he added five more. Then for 30 days he independently read 30 minutes every day, with me just checking in to see how he's doing. He now loves reading every morning for 30 minutes and talking about what he reads at breakfast. More of his friends are reading because he talked about great books he discovered. Now once a month, some of his friends and their moms (and dads) come over to talk about books and socialize.	*End*: On day 22, I tested my son to see if he would read without me. He didn't. So I ended up reminding him because his teacher says it's important that he read every night. I told him such, then set the timer and he started reading. Right now, he only reads when I remind him to read and set the timer. But when I don't, he just plays his video games. I don't know what to do anymore. I've tried everything, but he just doesn't like to read and will only do it if he has to. I'm worried I'm going to have to go to college with him.

Unfortunately, the mom in the race kept giving her son the fish to quicken the reading habit initiation process and instead she inadvertently made him dependent on her. He will now believe that reading happens outside of his control, and he'll always expect someone else to be responsible for his reading habit. When his mom left him out of the equation and took on all of the responsibility, she didn't make it possible for him to believe or have any skin in his reading game.

So what did the mom on the journey do different from the mom in the race?

1) She focused on gradually releasing responsibility to her son, ensuring his eventual independence with the habit.
2) She was willing and committed to support/guide/teach/and inspire as a coach and to model reading for him.
3) She began the initiation process believing that it was possible for her son to read for 30 minutes a day and she strategically worked backwards to ensure it.

4) With her son, she developed a plan that they both could live with and revised it when necessary during the weekly check-in chats.

5) She had daily, quality conversations about reading with her son and made the reading habit a pleasurable and social activity.

Feel ready now? I hope so! You have everything you need to confidently and peacefully instill the 30-minute-a day reading habit in your son.

Can't wait to see you again in the next book!

❦ ACKNOWLEDGMENTS ❧

This book wouldn't exist without the incredible support and love from my husband, Matt. With him, the sky's the limit.

Thank you to the incredible parents over the years (from 1991-2013) who trusted me and understood there was a "method to my madness." It was a true honor and privilege knowing and working with you and your sons.

Amy and Marlene, thank you for your support, friendship and believing in me.

During my years as an educator, I had the opportunity to learn from extraordinary and brilliant mentors: Drs. Carol (Gilmore) Dobish, Brenda Becker, Heidi Gross and Nancy Streim. Without their belief in my abilities, I would have given up on the education system many moons ago.

I want to thank Sheila Sydnor for always making sure kids had plenty of books to read; it made a huge difference in their lives.

I've been fortunate to have worked with and learned from awe-inspiring educators who went above and beyond for kids every day: Stacie Bardell, Hannah Bartges, Cindy Coppola, Jodi Gaudlip, Michele (Dixon) Gilbert, Doreen Hershey, Madelyn Riedel, and my favorite kindergarten trio (Mike, Penny and Melissa).

I was lucky to work with middle school teachers who knew the power of reading books: Chadd Johnson, Tarik Johnson, Julie Mikolajewski, Rich Staniec, and Megan Wapner.

Thank you to Marcia Tubin, an extraordinary educator, and advocate for kids, for being my first reader. Her excitement for what I wrote and belief in what I was saying are what kept me going through the tough parts.

Thank you to Claudia Svartefoss for stepping up to be my writing buddy and coach. Her enthusiasm, brilliance and willingness to share her knowledge about all things publishing and technology made my journey fun and my learning curve not as overwhelming. She also rocks it when it comes to building websites for non-techies like me (www.impactbee.com)!

Thank you to the wonderful and supportive people in my author/writer groups, Thor Svartefoss for my genius cover design, and Sara Zibrat for her extraordinary care in editing and formatting my book (it made all the difference).

❦ About the Author ❦

Hillary Tubin is the founder of Boy-Responsive Literacy Consulting, LLC, where she helps parents of self-proclaimed, non-reading 9- to 14-year-old boys instill the reading habit with confidence and harmony. After spending years figuring out why boys don't read and how to develop the mindset and create the environment so that they will read, Hillary is now determined to share what she learned with frustrated parents and educators so they can do the same.

Her hope is that aliterate boys and reading literacy becomes part of the national conversation like girls and math did in recent years.

When she's not advocating for boys and their future success in a global knowledge-based economy, Hillary loves to spend time with her husband, Matt, and two cats, Molly and Omar.

If you are interested or inspired to learn more about her coaching packages or school visits, please visit her website for further information: www.hillarytubin.com

✀ References ✀
(Endnotes)

1 "Kids and Family Reading Report, 5th Edition," Scholastic, 2015, accessed November 2015.

2 "The Common Sense Census: Media Use by Tweens + Teens," *Common Sense Media*, November 3, 2015, accessed November 2015.

3 "2015 Mathematics & Reading Assessments, Reading, Student Experiences 8th Grade," *Nation's Report Card,* 2015, accessed November 2015.

4 Margaret Kristin Merga, "How to Get Teenagers to Read," *The Conversation*, June 21, 2015, accessed November 2015.

5 "PISA 2012 results: The ABC of Gender Equality in Education: Aptitude, Behavior, Confidence: Chapter 2, Tackling underperformance among boys," *OECD*, (2015).

6 Alice Sullivan, "The Life-Long Benefits of Reading for Pleasure," *The School Librarian* 63, no. 1 (Spring 2015).

7 "NAEP 2012 Trends in Academic Progress, Reading 1971-2012, Mathematics 1973-2012, *The Nation's Report Card*, June 2013, accessed November 2015.

8 Ibid.

9 Ibid.

10 Marni Bromberg and Christina Theokas, "Meandering Toward Graduation: Transcript Outcomes of High School Graduates," (April 5, 2016), *The Education Trust*, accessed April 2016.

11 Adolescent Literacy: A Position Statement of the International Reading Association," *International Reading Association*, revised June 2012, accessed November 2015.

12 Tony Wagner, *The Global Achievement Gap: Why Even Our Best Schools Don't Teach the New Survival Skills Our Children Need—And What We Can Do About It* (Philadelphia: Basic Books, 2014), E-book.
13 Anne E. Cunningham and Keith E. Stanovich, "What Reading Does for the Mind," *Journal of Direct Instruction*, Vol. 1, No. 2, (Summer 2001).
14 Ibid.
15 Ibid.
16 Alice Sullivan and Matt Brown, "Vocabulary from adolescence to middle-age," *Institute of Education, University of London*, (November 2014).
17 Alice Sullivan and Matt Brown, "Reading for pleasure and attainment in vocabulary and mathematics," *Centre for Longitudinal Studies*, (April 2015).
18 David Comer Kidd and Emanuele Castano, "Reading Literary Fiction Improves Theory of Mind," *Sciencexpress*, October 3, 2013, accessed November 2015.
19 Neil Gaiman, "Why our future depends on libraries, reading and daydreaming," *The Guardian*, October, 15, 2013, accessed November 2015.
20 "Reading 'can help reduce stress'," *The Telegraph*, March 20, 2009, accessed November 2015.
21 "The Search for Alzheimer's Prevention Strategies," *NIH National Institute on Aging*, September 2012, updated February 1, 2016, accessed March 2016.
22 Tiffany Huges, Chung-Chou H. Chang, Joni Vander Bilt, Mary Ganguli, "Engagement in reading and hobbies and risk of incident dementia: The MoVIES Project," *Am J Alzheimers Dis Other Demen*, (August 2010).
23 John Coleman, "For Those Who Want to Lead, Read," *Harvard Business Review*, August 15, 2012, accessed March 2016.

24 Anne Kreamer, "The Business Case for Reading Novels," *Harvard Business Review*, January 11, 2012, accessed March 2016.

25 Ibid.

26 Tom Corley, "16 Rich Habits: Your autopilot mode can make you wealthy or poor," *Success.com*, October 8, 2014, accessed March 2016.

27 See note 1.

28 Amanda Ripley, *The Smartest Kids in the World: And How They Got That Way*, (New York: Simon & Schuster, 2013), E-book.

29 Ibid.

30 Michael Hyatt, "5 Ways Reading Makes You a Better Leader: The Science Behind Reading and Influence", *Michael Hyatt. com*, May 4, 2015, accessed March 2016.

31 Ibid.

32 Adele Faber and Elaine Mazlish, *How to Talk So Kids Will Listen & Listen So Kids Will Talk*, (New York: Scribner, 2012), E-book.

33 "American Time Use Survey Summary: Table 9 and 11," *Bureau of Labor Statistics*, June 24, 2015, accessed November 2015.

34 See note 1.

35 Anne E. Cunningham and Keith E. Stanovich, "What Reading Does for the Mind," *Journal of Direct Instruction*, Vol. 1, No. 2, (Summer 2001).

36 See note 2.

37 "PISA 2012 results: The ABC of Gender Equality in Education: Aptitude, Behavior, Confidence: Chapter 2, Tackling under-performance among boys, Excel figures," *OECD*, (2015).

38 See note 5.

39 See note 37.

40 Ibid.

41	Daniel J. Siegel, MD, *Brainstorm, The Power and Purpose of the Teenage Brain,* (New York: Penguin Group, 2013).

42	Sarah Spinks, "Adolescent Brains are Works in Progress," *Frontline, Inside the Teenage Brain,* accessed December 2015.

43	Interview Jay Giedd, *Frontline Inside the Teenage Brain,* accessed December 2015.

44	Gregory S. Berns, Kristina Blaine, Michael J. Prietula, and Brandon E. Pye, "Short-and Long-Term Effects of a Novel on Connectivity in the Brain," *Brain Connectivity* 3(6), December 1, 2013.

45	Jay Geibb, Interview, "Development of the Young Brain," *National Institute of Mental Health,* Transcript, May 2, 2011, accessed December 2015.

46	Ibid.

47	Ibid.

48	See note 5.

49	Richard Anderson, Paul T. Wilson, and Linda G. Fielding, "Growth in reading and how children spend their time outside of school," *Reading Research Quarterly,* Vol. 23, No. 3, (Summer, 1988).

50	See note 26.

51	See note 1.

52	See note 2.

53	William E. Nagy, Patricia A. Herman, Richard C. Anderson, "Learning Words from Context," Reading Research Quarterly, Vol. 20, No. 2, (Winter, 1985).

54	"Test Specifications for the Redesigned SAT," *College Board,* 2015, accessed March 2016.

55	See note 35.

56	Ibid.

57	"2015 Mathematics & Reading Assessments, Reading, Overall Achievement Levels 8th Grade," *The Nation's Report Card,* 2015, accessed November 2015.

58 "Reading Framework for the 2013 National Assessment of Educational Progress," *National Assessment Governing Board U.S. Department of Education*, October 2012, accessed November 2015.

59 See note 6.

60 Alice Sullivan and Matt Brown, "Social inequalities in cognitive scores at age 16: The role of reading," *Centre for Longitudinal Studies*, (September 2013), pdf.

61 "Adding ten minutes of reading time dramatically changes levels of print exposure," *Scientific Learning Reading Assistant*, March 2008, accessed November 2015.

62 James Kim, "Summer Reading and the Ethnic Achievement Gap," *Journal of Education for Students Placed at Risk* [Internet] 9(2), (2004).

63 Barbara Heyns, "Summer Learning and the Effects of Schooling," (New York: Academic Press, 1978).

64 "Ages & Stages, Teen," *American Academy of Pediatrics*, last updated November 21, 2015, accessed March 2015.

65 Clea McNeely and Jayne Blanchard, The Teen Years Explained: A Guide to Healthy Adolescent Development, *Johns Hopkins Bloomberg School of Public Health and Center for Adolescent Health*, 2009, accessed March 2015.

66 Charles Duhigg, *Power of Habit: Why We Do What We Do in Life and Business*, (New York: The Random House Publishing Group, 2012).

67 "Biography and Famous Quotes," *Vince Lombardi.com*, accessed February 2016.

.

7851

Made in the USA
Lexington, KY
07 February 2017